This book is dedicated to that
ecstatic feeling of finding a quicker,
easier way to do something.

ACKNOWLEDGEMENTS

I'd like to thank Dan Gookin for his pioneering work in computer journalism, and my wife, Tina, for helping me in more ways than I can possibly mention here. And my parents, too.

CONTENTS

INTRODUCTION   xi

PART 1: Master Your Operating System

CHAPTER 1: The MS-DOS Memory Mess   3
- Memory-Resident Programs   4
- High or Upper DOS Memory   6
- Expanded Memory   7
- Extended Memory   7
- Memory Managers   9
- Other Memory   10

CHAPTER 2: DOS Tips and Tricks   11
- The Big Boot   11
  - CONFIG.SYS   13
  - COMMAND.COM   14
  - AUTOEXEC.BAT   15
- Prompt   15
- PATH   16
- Batch Files   18
  - Pause the Directory   20
  - Changing File Dates   21

CHAPTER 3: Operating Systems   23
- UNIX   23
- OS/2   23
- *GeoWorks*   24
- *Windows*   24
  - Goo in Your Face   26
  - *Windows* Tricks and Tips   28
  - Customizing *Windows*   29
  - Extensions   30
  - Screenshots   31
  - UAE (Huh?)   32
  - Program Manager   33

PART 2: Shortcuts

CHAPTER 4: Utilities — 37

- CHKDSK.COM — 38
- LABEL.COM — 39
- MORE — 39
- SORT.EXE — 40
  - DIR |SORT — 40
  - DIR |SORT |MORE — 40
  - SORT < FILE.TXT — 40
  - SORT < FILE.TXT > FILESORT.TXT — 40
- DOS Version 5 — 41
  - Doskey — 41
  - Dosshell — 41
  - EDIT — 41
  - SETVER — 42
  - UNDELETE — 43
  - Other Utilities — 43

CHAPTER 5: Keyboard Tricks and Tips — 47

- Macros — 51
- Special Keys — 51
  - Esc — 52
  - Ctrl — 52
  - NumLock — 53
  - Ctrl-Alt-Del — 53
  - Scroll Lock — 53
  - SysRq — 53
  - CapsLock — 53
- Function Keys — 54
- Keyboard Tricks — 55
- Foreign Languages — 55
- ANSI.SYS — 56

PART 3: Hardware Hints

CHAPTER 6: Monitors 63
- Color Choices 64
  - CGA (Color Graphics Adapter) 64
  - EGA (Extended Graphics Adapter) 64
  - VGA (Video Graphics Array) 64
  - S-VGA (Super VGA) 64
- Monitor Facts 65
- Define Your Monitor Terms 66
- Trouble-Shooting 67
- Screen Savers 67
- Line Size 69

CHAPTER 7: Printers 71
- Dot Matrix Printers 71
- Impact Printers 73
- Inkjet Printers 73
- Thermal Printers 74
- Laser Printers 74
- Print Spoolers 76

CHAPTER 8: Expansion Boards 79
- Installing a Card 80
- Types of Cards 82
- Which Slot, Jack? 83
- Sound Cards 84
- Fax/Modems 85
- Scanners 85
- Memory Cards 86
- Video Cards 86
- Port Conflicts 86

PART 4: Fun and Finesse

CHAPTER 9: Modem Magic — 91

Computer Bulletin Board Systems — 92
  Prompt Dialing — 92
  What's the Cost? — 93
  Internal or External — 94
  Prodigy: A Commercial BBS With Commercials — 94
How to Make the First Call — 97

CHAPTER 10: Tips on Disks — 99

Floppy Disks — 99
Write-Protection — 100
Care and Feeding — 102
Hard Disks — 103
  Organizing Your Hard Drive — 103
  Help! I Deleted a File — 104
  Backups — 104
  Directories — 104
Compression Systems — 106

APPENDICES

APPENDIX A: All About ASCII Characters — 109

Control Characters — 109
Standard Text Characters — 110
Extended ASCII Characters — 110
Control Character Names — 111

APPENDIX B: Basic Command Set — 113

Modem Command Set — 113
S Registers — 117

APPENDIX C: Country CodePage Chart — 119

APPENDIX D: Telecommunications Services — 121

INDEX — 123

INTRODUCTION

When parking on a hill, turn your tires toward the curb. That way, if the brakes fail, your car will head for the sidewalk, not the middle of the road.

And don't slam on your brakes when you're driving on wet or icy roads; ease the pedal down with steady pressure until you come to a complete stop.

Nobody knows these driving tips when they first sit behind the steering wheel. They learn them through time and experience—and a little bit of high school driver's education.

It's the same way with personal computers, only more so because of the complexities involved. Cars merely drive from one place to another. Computers can do anything from checking your spelling to making animated videos.

Computers are much more complicated than automobiles, too. The keyboard contains more than 80 switches—more than you'll ever find on a dashboard. By pressing three keys simultaneously, the computer will head off in yet another direction. A car never requires the user to press the windshield wiper button and adjust the side mirror at the same time.

But when people sit down at a computer, they expect to learn it all, and quickly. This simply can't be done. Experience comes only through hands-on practice. And even the computer guru at the highest level will be stumped by some new command, or some new problem.

Luckily, books can help. This book gathers some of the most useful personal computer tips and tricks passed around through the years, and places them in one easy-to-read book. You'll find a thorough index in back, along with charts, graphs, and appendices.

You can read this book in one sitting for some general education, or refer to specific chapters to solve any particular problems at hand.

Hundreds of books have been written about the topics discussed here: DOS, printers, keyboards, *Windows*, utilities, and other computer gadgets. But by condensing the most useful and widespread computing tips, this guide will bring new levels of knowledge to just about every reader.

PART ONE

Mastering Your Operating System

CHAPTER 1

The MS-DOS Memory Mess

Here's the first big secret: You don't control your computer. DOS does, and you should be thankful.

The computer's Disk Operating System, usually known as MS-DOS, takes care all the detailed, messy computing chores you'd just as soon avoid. When you tell your computer to do something, you're really telling DOS to jump in there and make things happen.

The "MS" prefix stands for Microsoft, the same company that sells the flight simulator. Your IBM-compatible may be using MS-DOS, PC-DOS, or DR DOS, but each flavor of DOS does pretty much the same thing.

With DOS acting as coach, the computer quickly transforms your commands into numbers. It calculates the proper response, and returns with an intelligible answer. But to perform those vital calculations, the computer needs memory.

DOS controls the computer's pool of available memory, dishing it out to your computer's "brain," or CPU (Central Processing Unit), when needed. This memory is called Random-Access Memory, or RAM.

DOS then uses the RAM as a chalkboard to work out the needed calculations. When it's done, it pours the memory back into the pool, leaving it ready for the next task. If there's not enough memory for the task, DOS simply stops—often quite rudely, and at the worst possible moments.

The original PC could only grab memory from a potential pool of 1,024 kilobytes (K), and it could only use 640K of that RAM to run programs. That's not very much RAM by today's standards. But when created 10 years ago, IBM's PC was considered a short-lived fad, so it didn't receive much thought.

Unfortunately, that first PC created a standard that all other IBM compatibles have followed faithfully.

Although DOS can access 1,024K of memory, the first 640K chunk of RAM matters the most, as far we're concerned. It's called Conventional DOS memory, and it's the largest chunk of memory a single program can use. All DOS programs want that 640K badly, and most programs will use just about all of it. Even DOS stakes out a share for itself when your computer boots up; it steals anywhere from 19K to 75K of that 640K RAM total.

If your computer only has 512K, or, worse yet, 256K RAM, you won't have much RAM left over for programs at all. The original IBM PC only came with 64K! If you don't have 640K or more, don't be surprised when many programs won't load. Check the side of just about any software box; the fine print usually lists the required amount of RAM.

Memory-Resident Programs

Most programs load, run, and exit. But some programs load and sit there, waiting for another program to run alongside. That first embedded, or "resident," program in memory doesn't do anything until you touch a "hot key" to call it up. Then, it leaps to the forefront, ready for action.

The popular program *SideKick*, for instance, can bring an instant calendar to the screen when you press a certain key sequence, even if you're working in a word processor or other program. How does it work?

When *SideKick* is loaded, it grabs a chunk of the 640K of RAM, and just sits there in the background, taking up RAM space. Other

The MS-DOS Memory Mess

programs can come and go; *SideKick* stays put, constantly watching you type characters onto the keyboard. When the "hot key" sequence appears in the flow, *SideKick* "pops up" in a window on-screen, ready to perform its appointed task.

Memory-resident programs are known as TSRs because they load, Terminate, and Stay Resident. They should be called TCPs, though, because they often load, Terminate, and Cause Problems. TSRs are like Pet Rocks: Nobody really expected them, and no one knew what to do with them when they received one.

SECRET: Terminate, Stay Resident, and Cause Problems

Common TSRs include mouse drivers, sound card drivers, command line enhancements, notepads, and other goodies that remain loaded into your computer's memory.

If a new piece of software gives you trouble, try running it without loading any TSRs beforehand. The program might be not be comfortable sharing RAM with a TSR, and things could get ugly, fast.

If you usually load your TSR manually by typing in its name, then simply don't type it in. Then try running your problem program to see if that makes a difference. If it works fine, you've found your problem.

If your TSRs launch themselves automatically when you first turn on your computer, then they're probably hiding in your AUTOEXEC.BAT file.

To avoid this, perform a "clean" boot: Start your computer with a bootable, or "system" floppy disk in the A: drive. The computer looks to the A: drive first when starting up in the morning. If it finds a disk there, it will expect to find bootup instructions. (That's why your computer will freak out if there's a plain old data disk in there.)

A "system" floppy contains special instructions for your computer; any old floppy won't do. However, any old floppy can be converted to a "system" floppy. At the DOS prompt type "FORMAT A: /S" and the computer will format the disk, adding its special "bootup" instructions at the end. Be sure to use a new floppy disk, or one without any data on it, because the process renovates the disk, wiping it clean in the process.

The MS-DOS Memory Mess

DOS never expected TSRs, either. DOS expects programs to grab memory, perform, and then bail, dumping the RAM back into the pool, ready to be used by the next program.

So DOS often treats TSRs rudely, like uninvited strangers. DOS can accidentally let other programs bump into the portion of RAM held by a TSR, for instance, causing a fatal crash. Or one TSR can battle another TSR for the same portion of RAM.

High or Upper DOS Memory

As previously stated, Conventional DOS takes up 640K of the computer's 1,024K of usable RAM. The instructions that control the computer's hardware (the monitor, disk drives, etc.) head for that leftover 384K chunk of RAM, called High (or Upper) DOS memory because it sits above the conventional DOS's 640K.

When the PC was built, 640K RAM worked fine; it was 10 times as much memory as any other computer had at the time. Then spreadsheets entered the scene a few years

DOS Memory Map

The MS-DOS Memory Mess

later. Large companies wanted large spreadsheets, and all those calculations required more RAM than the 640K had to offer.

But Microsoft and IBM couldn't just come out with a new machine—they couldn't abandon the thousands of people who'd bought their earlier computers. So they started to piecemeal their way out of the situation.

Expanded Memory

When you run out of room on a large notepad, you begin taking notes on napkins, shuffling them around, hoping you can find them later. The computer does the same thing with "expanded memory."

To combat that lousy 640K memory barrier, some companies agreed to fasten some RAM chips onto a board, slide it into a slot inside their XT computers (see Chapter Eight), and call the new RAM "expanded memory." With the new memory came new rules about accessing it: the Expanded Memory Specification, or EMS.

The Expanded Memory Manager (EMM) grabbed a section of unused high DOS memory (where the hardware hangs out, remember?) and divvied it up into several "pages." When a program needed more memory to store information, the memory manager would shuttle the information to a blank page of high memory, rotate that newly filled page to the expanded memory board, and bring a fresh page to replace it. The memory manager repeated the process as needed, keeping track of all the pages, so it could shuffle the proper information back and forth when needed.

It works well, but there's a catch. Only EMS-sanctioned programs can use expanded memory. EMS-sanctioned programs are usually the big hoggy programs, so the combination works well. What if you don't have any EMS-compatible programs, and you've bought an EMS board at a swap meet? Then the board can still be used as a RAM drive, and that's not so bad at all.

Extended Memory

The next breed of computer contained a new chip, and some new technology along with it. Computers using the 80286 breed of chip

> **SECRET: Run a RAM Drive**
>
> Any memory above 640K can't be used by your programs unless you have an official EMS memory manager acting as "page director" to parcel it all out. But since few programs use EMS, the RAM usually just sits there, wasted.
>
> Turn that wasted memory into a RAM drive. A RAM drive can store information, just like a disk drive or a hard disk. Disk drives use motors to spin the disk so the drive heads can grab the stored information. (That's why they make a whirring sound.)
>
> Since RAM drives don't require mechanical motors, they're noticeably quicker than the fastest hard disk, and very much faster than a disk drive. The phrase "lightning quick" comes to mind. (They're also silent.)
>
> For instance, instead of running a program off a floppy (and twiddling your thumbs while the drive makes grinding noises as it searches for data), copy that program to a RAM disk and run it there. Copy the data to your RAM drive, and you'll be moving even faster.
>
> Different versions of DOS use different RAM disk installers, but they work in a similar way. To make a 360K RAM drive from my extended memory using DOS 3.3, I added the following line to my CONFIG.SYS file:
>
> DEVICE=C:\DOS\RAMDRIVE.SYS 360 /A
>
> Check your DOS manual; you might need to substitute the word VDISK.SYS (Virtual Disk) for RAMDRIVE.SYS, depending on your version of DOS. Also, the "A" stands for "expanded memory." Use the letter "E" instead if you're using an AT or a '386 with "extended memory" (see next section).
>
> When you've changed your CONFIG.SYS file, reboot your computer. When it wakes up again, it will have an extra disk drive listed on the directory.

(and its successors, the '386 and '486) can access a lot more RAM than the piddling XT. It's not uncommon to hear of '386 machines with about 8,000K, or 8 megabytes (MB), of RAM. Extra memory in these types of computers is called "extended memory."

The MS-DOS Memory Mess

Extended memory chips plug right into the computer's motherboard, whereas expanded memory can only fit on a card that plugs into a slot.

Instead of being parcelled out in small pages like expanded memory, extended memory lines up in one big strip, ready to jump into action if a program needs more than 640K of RAM.

But there's a problem: DOS can't use extended memory, even though it's sitting right there, built into the motherboard. The computer can use it, but only with other operating systems or environments, like UNIX, Xenix, OS/2, or *Windows* (see Chapter Three). Those operating systems force the chip to run in a special "Enhanced Mode," so it can use the extended memory.

But in order to run DOS programs, those powerful chips have to slip back into "Real Mode," a mode which emulates the earlier computers (and their 640K limitation on accessible RAM). It's a mess.

So, to use extended memory, DOS falls back on the same old trick: It treats *extended memory* like *expanded memory*, and pulls the same old page-swapping technique for those special EMS-aware DOS programs. But cheer up. You can use extended memory as a RAM disk, just like before.

Memory Managers

Here's a big secret: DOS can't use the extended memory, but a memory manager can. Several years ago, an upstart company called Quarterdeck released a revolutionary product called *QEMM* (Quarterdeck Expanded Memory Manager) that lets you put all your computer's memory to work.

QEMM first searches every inch of your computer for all possible RAM locations. It looks in your high or upper memory for any leftover memory, and converts it to expanded memory. This previously inaccessible RAM can now be filled with other goodies like TSRs or device drivers (see Chapter Two), leaving more of that ever-so-important 640K chunk for the programs.

After identifying all possible storage sites, and locating any extended memory on the motherboard, *QEMM* converts all the RAM into expanded memory, ready to be paged out to the computer when needed for storage or extra calculations.

Why can't DOS do this all by itself? Too much work, I guess, although the latest version makes an effort. MS-DOS version 5.0 is the first DOS version not to load itself into the 640K RAM. Instead, it grabs a "footprint" of about 20K, then sticks the rest of itself into extended memory. That DOS 5.0 trick only works if you have a computer from the '286 family (with at least 64K of extended memory to go with it). And it still won't let programs use your extended memory, as *QEMM* does.

Do you still own an older, XT computer? Then MS-DOS version 5.0 will remain in the precious 640K of RAM, giving users one more reason to upgrade.

Other Memory

Your computer might have other memory options, as well, but we'll talk about that in Chapter Eight.

CHAPTER 2

DOS Tips and Tricks

Memory just kind of sits there and records information. Besides buying a memory manager, there's not much you can do to make the process easier. But DOS is a different story. You'd better make friends with DOS because it's the interpreter between you and your computer.

Secrets? Bunches of 'em. Just like you should remember to tip Moscow taxi drivers with Marlboros, you should remember a few things to make your computing trips easier and less expensive.

Microsoft has released more than five versions of DOS, and tossed in a thick book with each of them. Here, we'll just discuss a few secrets about how DOS works, and how you can make it work harder for you. But before you can put the secrets to work, you have to understand how DOS itself works.

The Big Boot

When you turn on your computer in the morning, a jolt of electricity runs through its chips, pulling them to life. The computer wakes up, and begins looking around to see who it is, what hardware it's attached to, and what it's supposed to do.

Just as people can write permanent notes on paper, programmers can write permanent instructions on a computer chip. But not on

RAM chips; they lose their memory when the computer is turned off. ROM (Read-Only Memory) chips keep their instructions forever. When the computer first turns on, it looks at its ROM chips, where the manufacturer has stored its first few start-up instructions. The instructions are called BIOS (Basic Input/Output System).

With BIOS in hand, the computer gives itself a brief RAM chip test, then looks for a disk in the A: drive containing more detailed loading instructions. If it can't find the information on a disk in the A: drive, you've seen the results:

Non-System disk or disk error
Replace and strike any key when ready

Most people have a hard disk, so the computer will look there for information if there's nothing in the A: drive. The computer's looking for some sneaky invisible files to put its internal affairs in order. When it finds those files, it searches for the CONFIG.SYS file.

Secret: ROM Madness

Programmers can store anything they want into ROM, and some of it runs to the extreme. Programmers can install a "back door," which is an undocumented command that often does something frivolous.

For instance, sit in front of a Macintosh SE, and boot it up. When you see the "Welcome to Macintosh" sign, hold down the "programmer's key," the plastic switch on the Mac's left-hand side, closest to the rear. You'll see a ">" symbol on-screen. Type "G 41D89A" and hit the <Enter> key. You'll see a picture of the Macintosh's programming team on the screen. That digitized photo has been hidden in ROM by a sneaky programmer.

Or, while your Amiga boots, hold down both <Shift> keys and both <Alt> keys. While holding down those four keys, hit any of the Function keys, and you'll see a hidden message for each one.

What are the DOS secret back doors? There aren't any. Remember, it's a Serious Business Machine. Straighten your tie.

> **SECRET: Sneaky Invisible Files**
>
> To avoid confusing people, DOS stores some of its starting-up instructions under wraps. MS-DOS uses two invisible files called IO.SYS and MSDOS.SYS. Normally, you'll never see these files, and you'll never have to deal with them: They work automatically. But if you do see them, for whatever reason, don't erase 'em. They're important.
>
> Here's the secret: When you make a bootable floppy on a 360K disk, the COMMAND.COM file takes up about 25K of space (at least that's how big version 3.3 is, and as they say on TV, "your version may vary"). With 360K total space, and 25K devoted to one file, the disk should have 335K space left. But it doesn't; there's only 252K. Where'd the extra space go?
>
> It's taken up by the sneaky invisible files, that's where. And there's no way to get around it. And don't erase COMMAND.COM, either. Your computer needs that, too.

CONFIG.SYS

This simple text file gives the computer even *more* loading instructions; you usually don't have to worry about it. In fact, your computer will often work fine even if the file doesn't exist. Some programs will add a few lines to your CONFIG.SYS file so your computer will react to things in a certain manner. If these programs can't find an existing CONFIG.SYS file, they may create one for you.

Your CONFIG.SYS file can contain a driver telling the computer how to deal with a mouse, for instance. Or it can tell DOS to use a foreign country's method of displaying time, date and currency. It can create a RAM drive, as discussed in Chapter One. Or it can tell DOS what devices it has to play with: video displays, network instructions, and other goodies.

Since CONFIG.SYS is a text file, you'll have to observe some precautions if you decide to change it. Use a text editor, like the one that comes with DOS 5.0. If you don't have a text editor, use your word processor, but save the file in ASCII format (a simple text file stripped of any special codes). Check your word processor's manual (or menu) for the correct way to load and save an ASCII file.

Finally, reboot your computer. It only reads the CONFIG.SYS file once, and that's when it first boots up. If you don't reboot, it will never know you've been fiddling with the CONFIG.SYS file.

SECRET: ASCII Files

Don't know if you have an ASCII file or not? Your word processor might already be creating them. To check, use the DOS command "TYPE FILENAME". (Substitute the name of your file for the word "FILENAME", of course.) Then, watch as the file's contents scroll across your screen. If words, letters, sentences, or paragraphs flow by in a fairly orderly manner, the file is an ASCII file. If you hear erratic beeps or the text contains weird, unrecognizable characters, the file isn't a straight ASCII file.

The TYPE command can peek inside any file, but with limited results. If you peek into enough command files (they end with the letters COM), you'll eventually see the "smiley face" character. It's not only a weird, unrecognizable character, it shows you from what era the computer's programmers came.

COMMAND.COM

After the computer finds the CONFIG.SYS file, it looks for a file named COMMAND.COM. Whenever your system creates a bootable floppy, it tosses COMMAND.COM onto the disk. This is the program that reads the commands you type in at the DOS prompt.

Whenever a program ends, the computer returns to and loads the COMMAND.COM file, so it will know how to handle your next command-line instruction, whether it's a command like "DIR" or another program name. If you've booted your computer off a floppy, you'll have to stick the COMMAND.COM disk back into the disk drive, because DOS always looks for COMMAND.COM in the last place it was found. If you're booting off a hard drive, the process is so quick and automatic it's almost invisible.

DOS Tips and Tricks *15*

AUTOEXEC.BAT

After reading the ROM chips, the secret invisible files, the CONFIG.SYS file, and the COMMAND.COM file, (whew . . .) the computer ends its journey by looking for a program named AUTOEXEC.BAT. This is where most of your own handiwork will take place. (Finally!)

You can add tasks to this file so your computer will execute them automatically (hence the file name AUTOEXEC.BAT) when it starts up. For instance, let's say you want your computer to automatically load a program when you turn it on.

Add the command to the bottom of your AUTOEXEC.BAT file. For instance, if you normally type "WIN" in the morning to start up Microsoft *Windows*, add the short, single line "WIN" to the bottom of your AUTOEXEC.BAT file. Your computer will automatically begin running *Windows* when you first turn it on.

Prompt

Here's a big secret: You don't always have to look at that same prompt, those characters that appear on the command line.

People with a hard drive usually see this prompt:

C:\>

That's because their AUTOEXEC.BAT file contains the phrase "PROMPT= pg" somewhere inside. (Use the command "TYPE AUTOEXEC.BAT" and see what's inside your own AUTOEXEC.BAT file.) The "$p" tells the computer to display your current path (more about paths, later) at the prompt. The "=" sign is optional, by the way. If you move to another directory, for example the "Book" directory, your prompt will look like this:

C:\BOOK>

The "$g" tells your computer to add the ">" sign, so it looks like everybody else's prompt.

You can customize your prompt to reflect your own weird

desires. I knew one guy who turned his prompt into a simple "." by using the command: "PROMPT=." That way no onlookers could see what directory he was in. Paranoid? Yes.

Anyway, here's a chart of what different symbols will do to your prompt:

Command	Displays
$$	$ (the dollar sign)
$b	| (known as a "pipe")
$d	the current date
$e	^[(the Escape character)
$g	> (greater than)
$h	destructive backspace (deletes the character to its left)
$l	< (less than)
$n	the current drive letter
$p	the current pathname (subdirectory)
$q	= (the equals sign)
$t	the current time
$v	the version of DOS
$_	a carriage return

PATH

DOS follows a specific path when it's trying to locate files. Like anybody else, DOS looks in the closest place first; that means the path is normally the directory you're currently visiting. If you type GO, for instance, DOS will search your current directory for the program named GO. If it's not there, it gives up.

What if you're in your C:\WORDS directory, and you want to access a program in your C:\UTILITY directory? From the WORDS directory, you'd type \UTILITY\GO.

That shows DOS the correct path from the WORDS directory to the UTILITY directory. Now DOS will be able to find the file, and run it, staying in the same directory.

Why didn't you have to type "C:\UTILITY\GO"? Because when you don't type anything before that first "\", DOS assumes the path extends from the root directory, or the basic "C:\>" prompt.

DOS Tips and Tricks

> **SECRET: Prompt Prompts**
>
> When you want to start fiddling around with your own prompts, check out the following. Just type them in at your current DOS prompt. If you like them, add the command to your AUTOEXEC.BAT file.
>
> | Command | Displays |
> | --- | --- |
> | Prompt=pg | C:\> |
> | Prompt=Yes, Master? | Yes, Master? |
> | Prompt=d_ thhhhhh_ pg | Thu 8-08-91 13:40 C:\BOOK |
> | Prompt=Think Positive.$_ pg | Think Positive. C:\BOOK |
>
> After reading Chapter Five (and installing your ANSI.SYS driver accordingly), start using the $e command to add some color, or even animation to your prompt. It's fun and easy to fiddle around with prompts, especially if you're trying to put off a boring project.

Here's a secret: You can give DOS a predetermined path to follow automatically when it boots up. That way it can find your favorite files automatically, from anywhere on your hard drive. To do this, put a PATH statement in your AUTOEXEC.BAT file. For instance, look at the following path statement:

PATH C:\UTILITY;C:\DOS;D:\C:\UTILITY;D:\C:\DOS

Now, when I type a program name, DOS first looks in the current directory. If it can't find it, it runs to the UTILITY directory on drive C: and looks there, then it looks in the DOS directory. Only then does it stop searching. The "D:\" prefixes mean that DOS will search those directories on C: even if I'm in a directory on the D: drive.

To find out your current path, type PATH from any DOS prompt. If you haven't set up a path, you won't see any directories listed after the word PATH. But if you've set one up in your AUTOEXEC.BAT file, it'll appear on-screen.

You can change your PATH at any time by typing a new "PATH=" command at the command line.

To make things simpler, should you put *all* your directories on the path? No, because it slows things down. If you accidentally type "GE" instead of "GO", DOS won't know you messed up. It will look through every directory on the path, frantically searching for the GE program before returning to the prompt. On a slow computer, it can take a *long* time.

Instead, there's an even easier way to launch files from anywhere in your directory. It's called a batch file, and it's a powerful secret to power computing.

Batch Files

Batch files can revolutionize the way you use your computer, so listen closely.

Computers work best when they're repeating things. Humans usually find it tiresome to type the same thing over and over, but DOS doesn't care. So whenever you find yourself typing the same commands at the DOS prompt, consider a batch file.

A batch file is a text file, just like the CONFIG.SYS and AUTOEXEC.BAT files. In fact, AUTOEXEC.BAT is a batch file. You can tell because it ends with the extension BAT. A batch file is a collection of commands that you'd normally type at the DOS prompt.

The commands have been collected and saved as a text file with the extension BAT. Here's a collection of commands I saved under the name READCHAP.BAT to form the READCHAP batch file:

```
c:
cd \book\chapter1
type chapter1.txt
```

Now, when I type "READCHAP", DOS will look for the batch file READCHAP (following any predetermined path) and run it. When READCHAP.BAT executes, it tells DOS to move to the C: drive, then move to the subdirectory CHAPTER1 under the BOOK

DOS Tips and Tricks

directory. Then it will TYPE the contents of the CHAPTER1.TXT file to the screen.

Instead of putting all your programs on your path, it's better to write batch files to run them. For instance, here's my batch file to load *Windows*:

```
c:
prompt {Windows} $p$g
cd \windows
win
cd\
prompt $p$g
cls
```

This causes the computer to change to the *Windows* directory, and run *Windows*. But what's that prompt stuff doing in there? That's a secret that's going to get its own box, right down below.

SECRET: Don't Shell Yourself Short

Some programs, like *Windows*, allow you to "shell to DOS." That simply means the program will leave the screen, sit in the background, and give you a DOS prompt so you can perform other tasks.

While in the shell, you can move files around, create directories, or even start other programs (as long as you have enough RAM). A shell looks just like a regular DOS prompt. And that's the problem: You can forget the first program that's sitting patiently in RAM, waiting for you to leave its shell and come back.

If you accidentally try to load that first program from within its own shell, it'll cause problems. It might load, but work very slowly, making you wonder what's wrong. Or it might crash outright.

To avoid this problem, change your DOS prompt before loading the program. For instance, before loading *Windows*, change your prompt to say "{Windows} C:\>". That way you'll never forget you're in a shell from *Windows*, and that you're not really in DOS.

To make the process easier, put the prompt information in the batch file that calls the program. Then you'll never forget.

Batch files can be much more than a collection of DOS commands. It's actually a programming language of sorts. But now that you know the basics, you can find the other stuff on your own.

How do you make batch files if you don't have a text editor, and your word processor can't save files as ASCII text (or it just doesn't know how to save 'em that way)? Try this next trick:

SECRET: Copy CON, Captain!

If you need to create a small ASCII file in a hurry, try this trick. You don't need an editor or a word processor.

To create a batch file called TEST.TXT, go to the DOS prompt, type "COPY CON TEST.TXT <Enter>", then start typing your commands. When you're finished, type <Ctrl-Z>. It'll look like this:

```
COPY CON TEST.TXT <Enter>
Dear Uncle Ebeneezer, <Enter>
Please send money very quickly. <Enter>
I want to buy some more RAM chips for my computer. <Enter>
Thanks very much, <Enter>
Cousin Andy <Enter>
^Z <Enter>
```

At the end, when you type ^Z and <Enter>, DOS saves your text to the file TEST.TXT. Type DIR and see for yourself. Then type TYPE TEST.TXT and watch your new letter scroll across your screen. To print it, turn on your printer and type "COPY TEST.TXT PRN".

DOS will copy your newly formed text file to your printer. Now, don't you feel foolish for spending hundreds of dollars on a word processor?

DOS comes with a bunch of built-in commands; you'll never use many of them. But here are a few common tricks:

Pause the Directory

When you type "DIR", DOS responds with a list of file names, their size, and the time they were created. If it scrolls past too quickly, type "DIR /p, and DOS will give you a screenful of names, then pause so you can read 'em. Hit any key for the next page.

For a wide directory (one that wraps into several columns), type "DIR /w", and for a wide directory that pauses, type "dir /p/w". [Note: Throughout this book, type what's inside the quotation marks, not the quotation marks themselves. When you see a word within "<>" marks, like <Enter>, that means to press the key marked "Enter."]

Changing File Dates

When you type DIR, DOS lists the dates the files were created. If you want to change the file MYFILE.TXT to the current date, use this command:

```
COPY MYFILE.TXT +,,
```

The next time you type DIR, you'll see that the new date has replaced the old. Want to give it a different date? Then type DATE at the DOS prompt, and type in the date you want. Then type the above COPY command. That's it. Oh, remember to change the date back to reality when you're through with your little time warp.

CHAPTER 3

Operating Systems

IBM-compatible computers don't necessarily have to run MS-DOS. Several alternative operating systems, like PC-DOS or DR DOS, do almost the same thing, with just a few slight differences.

IBM-compatibles don't have to run DOS at all. The real differences come when using operating systems like UNIX, Xenix, OS/2, and *Windows* (actually, *Windows* is an "environment"... you'll learn more in the next few paragraphs.)

UNIX

Originally developed by the phone company to handle vast volumes of files, UNIX once ran on large, mainframe computers and high-powered workstations. It uses different commands than DOS to accomplish similar computing tasks; it can also handle more than one user at the same time.

Xenix is a version of UNIX specifically designed for IBM-compatible computers. Unless you're a hard-core computer user, leave UNIX alone.

OS/2

This is IBM's baby, and it hasn't caught on enough to warrant more than a mention here. Just remember it looks almost like

Windows, but can directly address your extended memory, making it better for some applications. Still, if you don't know what it is, you probably don't need it.

GeoWorks

This operating system runs on top of DOS, but lets programs run in "pop-up" windows on the screen. In fact, it's very similar to *Windows*, mentioned below. It hit the market after *Windows*, so it hasn't really caught on. For this reason, we're not going to go into it in depth.

Windows

Now, we're talking turkey. *Windows* 3.0 caught fire in 1990, although it had already been around for five years. In the mid-'80s, *Windows* brought pictures instead of words to MS-DOS computers.

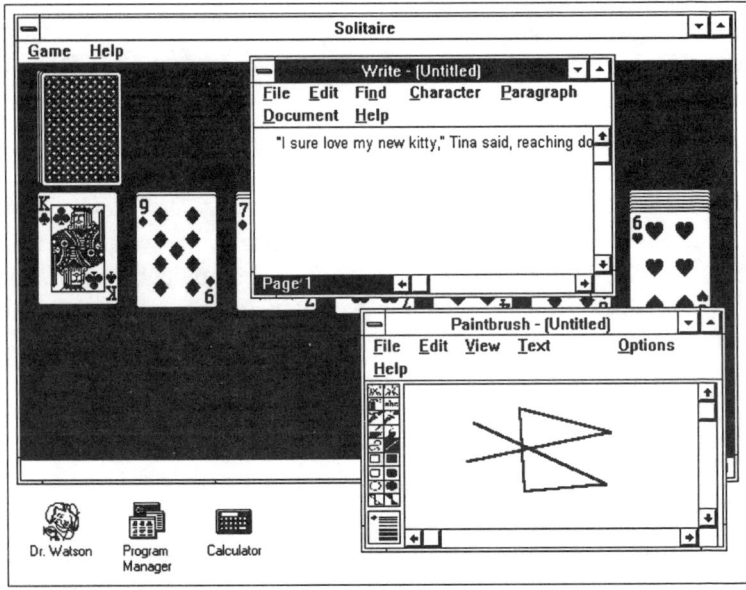

Windows *at work. (Notice the game in the background!)*

Operating Systems

Instead of typing in program names, users could start a program by using a mouse to click on pictures.

The program pops onto the screen inside a "window." You can move the window around, or change its size. You can run other programs alongside it, each in its own window. This makes it easy to use a word processor to take notes about your spreadsheet, for instance.

But *Windows* is more than pretty pictures. It comes with two word processors, a card file for storing phone numbers, a paint program, a telecommunications program, and a few other goodies. It's easy to grab information from one window and stick it into another.

Perhaps most important, *Windows* brings its own memory manager to the PC. Unlike DOS, *Windows* can use any extended memory (memory more than 640K) in your computer. On a '386 computer, it will even convert part of your hard drive into extra memory. But it can only run *Windows*-sanctioned programs using that extended memory.

You see, *Windows* doesn't replace DOS, it operates on top of DOS. That means when you use *Windows* to run DOS programs (sticking them in their own window), you're stuck with the same old 640K barrier. Luckily, plenty of companies have embraced

---

SECRET: A DOS of *Windows*

Windows takes over your computer completely; you'll never have to mess with another DOS command. Unless you want to, of course. *Windows*, like other programs, lets you shell to DOS: The DOS prompt runs inside its own window, or it can completely fill the screen.

But don't bother running any DOS programs under *Windows*. They might work, but they'll be slow. And you'd be missing the whole point of *Windows*: the interaction between *Windows* programs.

So either dump DOS for *Windows*, or dump *Windows* and stay with DOS. But don't try to combine the two environments.

Windows, so you can probably find a new *Windows* version of a program that performs just as well as your old DOS version.

Like Macintosh programs, most *Windows* programs have a similar "look and feel." They all "cut and paste" to a single clipboard. Information grabbed off the screen from the telecommunications program, for instance, can be pasted into a text file, and then embellished with pieces of artwork from the paint program.

Using *Windows*' "Dynamic Data Exchange," an *Excel* spreadsheet can be "dynamically" pasted into a *Word* for *Windows* document. Whenever you change your spreadsheet's numbers, your text document will be updated automatically. You can even have the telecom program automatically grab numbers through the modem, and dump them into the spreadsheet, which in turn dumps the updated graph into the document or report.

It sounds nifty, but there's some bad news: *Windows* won't run on a traditional XT. It's sluggish on an AT, although the box says it'll work on an AT with 640K memory. The box also says it will work with a keyboard, but realistically, you need a mouse.

And for sharp, readable resolution, you'll need a high-quality VGA card and monitor. Don't forget the hard drive, either. *Windows* takes up a few megs itself, and to use the expanded memory scheme, you'll want at least 4 MB of free hard disk space after *Windows* has been installed.

In fact, some people say not to bother running *Windows* on anything less than a VGA '386 with at least 2 megs of extended memory. So although *Windows* retails for $149 ($99 street price), the hardware investment runs much higher.

Without the added memory, you'll only be able to open a few windows at the same time, hampering the program's effectiveness.

Goo in Your Face

Windows is a GUI (pronounced "gooey"), meaning a Graphical User Interface. It's graphical in that it uses pictures, not words, to represent programs and commands.

But since GUIs rely on graphics to make their point, they're usually slower than comparable DOS programs.

Some GUIs require an all-or-nothing commitment: Either you use *only* programs written for that GUI, or you don't use any one of them. It doesn't make sense to install *Windows* (and have it devour a good percentage of your hard drive) if you only want to run one or two *Windows* applications.

Before switching to a GUI, ask yourself a few questions:

- Will a GUI help me perform my current work faster or with better quality?

- Do I have a powerful enough machine, or will I have to buy more expensive equipment?

SECRET: Where's My Wallpaper?

Forget the programs. How do you change wallpaper? It's easy, and it introduces you to one of *Windows'* most important files: WIN.INI.

Find the Control Panel icon in your Program Manager window, and give it a double-click with the mouse. When the control panel pops up, double-click on the "desktop" icon. When that pops up, look for the word "Wallpaper," and click on the small, downward-pointed black arrow.

Yet another window will pop up, this time containing names of wallpaper files. Any file with the extension .BMP can be used for wallpaper. For instance, the *Paint* program saves files with a BMP extension, so anything you create in *Paint* can be used for wallpaper.

Click on the file name you want, then double-click on the square in the top, left-hand corner of the Desktop's window. It will disappear, your wallpaper will change, and you'll see the Control Panel window sitting there where you left it. Double-click on the square in the top, left-hand corner of the Control Panel's window (that's how you get rid of *any* window in *Windows*), and you're through.

Yay! (It's a lot easier than it sounds, trust me.)

- Am I willing to give up my favorite DOS programs in favor of learning new programs in a new environment?
- Do I have the time to sit down and learn a completely new and different way of using my computer?
- What sort of software will run under that GUI?

If you still want to proceed, go for it. You can always switch back.

Windows *Tricks and Tips*

The first thing you'll notice is all the colors in *Windows*. *Windows* lets you decorate your computer screen in many ways. The most noticeable comes with *Windows*' wallpaper. *Windows* decorates the back of your screen with pretty colors or pictures; once you've laid down your wallpaper, you put your windows over it.

Before you go wild with your wallpaper, here's a secret: It uses a *lot* of memory, and can really slow *Windows* down. Unless you have plenty of RAM (four megs or more), try to limit your artistic creations to less than 30K apiece. Try making small pictures, then using the "tile" command to spread them across your screen.

Best yet, use the desktop's "pattern" command to add textured color as wallpaper. That takes barely any memory at all.

If you're not going to be using the BMP wallpaper files that came with *Windows*, delete them from your hard drive. Remember, when

---

SECRET: The Handy System Editor

Windows comes with a nifty program called SYSEDIT.EXE. This is a fancy version of a notebook-style editor, and it automatically brings up four files: AUTOEXEC.BAT, CONFIG.SYS, SYSTEM.INI and WIN.INI.

The editor's a secret; you won't find it listed in the *Windows* manual. But it's very handy for quickly editing any or all of these files. Make an icon for it on your Program Manager, so you'll have quick access to it.

Operating Systems 29

using a '386 with *Windows*, it uses your hard drive as memory; keep it clean of unneeded files.

You can customize the windows themselves to meet your tastes. For instance, the "color" button on the control panel lets you change the color of the windows' borders and menus. Feel free to fiddle; it's the best way to learn.

Customizing Windows

Just as your AUTOEXEC.BAT file can tell DOS what to do when it boots up, you can tell *Windows* what to do by customizing its WIN.INI file. Use Notepad or SYSEDIT to bring your WIN.INI file to the screen. The first thing you'll see under the word "Windows" is the phrase, "load="

Mine, for instance, looks like this:

load=cards.crd,time.exe,browser.exe,saver.exe,macros.rec,stars.exe

That line tells *Windows* what files to open when it first starts up. It'll load my address book, a clock, a browser utility, a screen saver, my macro file, and the program "STARS.EXE."

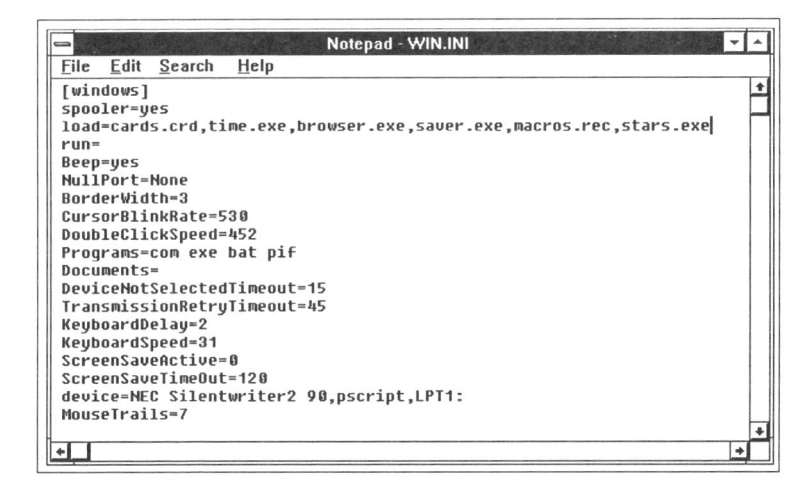

```
Notepad - WIN.INI
File  Edit  Search  Help
[windows]
spooler=yes
load=cards.crd,time.exe,browser.exe,saver.exe,macros.rec,stars.exe
run=
Beep=yes
NullPort=None
BorderWidth=3
CursorBlinkRate=530
DoubleClickSpeed=452
Programs=com exe bat pif
Documents=
DeviceNotSelectedTimeout=15
TransmissionRetryTimeout=45
KeyboardDelay=2
KeyboardSpeed=31
ScreenSaveActive=0
ScreenSaveTimeOut=120
device=NEC Silentwriter2 90,pscript,LPT1:
MouseTrails=7
```

Here's a WIN.INI file, ready to be customized.

Windows grabs the files listed after the "load=" statement and puts them at the bottom of the screen as icons, waiting to be "clicked" into action. After changing your WIN.INI file, save it, exit *Windows*, and restart for the changes to be effective.

Extensions

From the start, DOS recognizes three file name extensions: EXE, COM and BAT. Same with *Windows*. If you double-click on any name with those extensions, it'll run the program.

You can make *Windows* do a lot more, however, with the following secret: In your WIN.INI file, further down from the "load=" statement, you'll see the word "extensions." When you're using File Manager, and you click on a file with the extension TXT, *Windows* loads "Notepad," and opens that file. Why? Because TXT has been linked to the program NOTEPAD.EXE in the extensions section.

Here's what it looks like:

[Extensions]
txt=notepad.exe ^.txt

SECRETS: Move Over, Mouse

Windows works best with a mouse, no doubt about it. But sometimes the keyboard can be quicker than finding the mouse, moving it to the top of the menu, clicking and pulling down the menu, and clicking on the appropriate command. To save time, here's the keyboard equivalent of a few commonly used commands:

<Ctrl-Ins> Copy highlighted information to clipboard.

<Shift-Ins> Paste clipboard information into application.

< Alt-Spacebar> Brings up the current window's Control Menu (when faced with a long list of file names in a menu, press the first letter of the desired file; the cursor will jump there.)

<Ctrl-Esc> The same as double-clicking on the background, it brings up the Task Manager to swap programs.

<F1> Brings up that program's help menu.

You can add your own extensions by using the same syntax. Then, when you double-click on a file name with that extension, Notepad will automatically load up with that file.

If you add this line, for instance:

```
nts=notepad.exe ^.nts
```

you can then click on any file ending in ".NTS" and it will come to the screen inside Notepad.

Screenshots

Remember how difficult it could be to take a screenshot, a "snapshot" of your screen, when running a DOS program? You'd have to load some memory-resident screen-capture utility, and hope the two programs wouldn't battle each other.

Windows, being a graphics environment, makes it easy to take a screenshot. Just arrange the window the way you want it, then press <Shft-PrtSc>. The <PrtSc> key is the "Print Screen" key, and it's found on almost all keyboards (although it rarely works properly with DOS applications).

Now, call up *Windows*' Clipboard, and voila! You'll see your snapshot on the clipboard, ready to be pasted into other applications.

SECRETS: The Real Secrets

Pssssst. Wanna hear some real secrets? This is the stuff *Windows* didn't tell you about in the manual. They're the "back doors" we talked about in Chapter Two.

From anywhere in *Windows* 3.0, hold down the <F3> key, type WIN3, release <F3>, and hit the <Backspace> key. You'll see what the 3.0 development team wanted you to have for wallpaper.

Load the *Windows* game *Solitaire* under "timed" mode, choose the palm tree deck of cards, and watch the sun. He'll stick his tongue out once every minute. Check for the hidden animations in the other decks of cards, too. They only appear when in the "timed" mode.

You can even call it into *Paint* and save it as a BMP file, ready to be used as wallpaper. But that would be rather confusing. Which icons are real, and which are simply wallpaper?

If you just want a screenshot of one particular window, move there and type <Alt-PrtSc>.

UAE (Huh?)

The term UAE refers to Unrecoverable Application Error, and if you use *Windows* long enough, you'll see one. The error message doesn't mean you've done something wrong. It means *Windows* has a few bugs. A bug refers to a flaw in a computer or program that makes the computer stop working. The term started when a moth

---

SECRET: Sharing Files

Windows thrives on having bunches of programs and files sitting on your screen at the same time. Let's say you open a Notepad file called NOTES.TXT. You add a brilliant thought about a new brand of potato chips, then shrink the file to an icon at the bottom of your screen.

An hour later, in the throes of creative inspiration, you forget that you've already opened NOTES.TXT. Instead of using the shrunken icon at the bottom of the file, you open the NOTES.TXT file from your hard drive, effectively creating a new version of the file. You type in another brilliantly marketable idea, save the file, and shrink it down to the bottom of the screen.

At the end of the day, you notice you have two versions of NOTES.TXT sitting on the bottom of your screen. Oh, no! Now you have to open both of them, compare the contents, and decide which version is more recent. It's a headache, and it's avoidable.

Simply put the word SHARE on a separate line in your AUTO-EXEC.BAT file. Normally used for network applications, SHARE monitors which files are being used. If you try to open a file that's already open, DOS will stop you, telling you to wise up and pay attention.

It's a great way to keep from accidentally dropping ideas out an already open window.

Operating Systems *33*

flew into a computer and died, and the term is used when something is making programs run oddly.

You'll have to live with UAEs until all the bugs fly out of *Windows*. Since it's such a complex program (it's a complete operating system that rides on top of yet another complete operating system), you'll probably see bugs popping up every so often. Actually, it's a good thing: It will force you to save your work often, which you should be doing anyway.

Windows 3.1 does a better job of handling UAEs, but they're still there.

Program Manager

Don't lose your bottom row of icons by making your program manager fill the entire screen. Instead, double-click on your wallpaper (or hit <Ctrl-Esc> to call up the Task Manager. Hit "Tile" when Program Manager is the only open window, and it will automatically align itself to the right proportions.

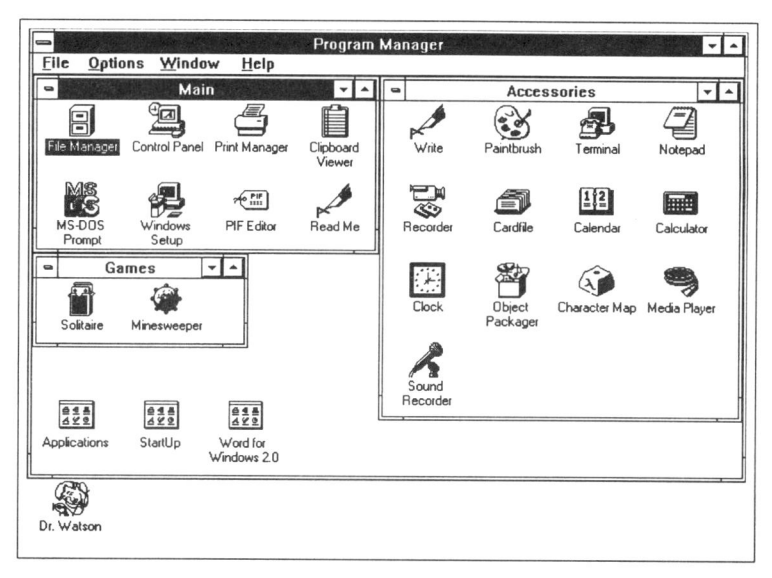

Windows *with Program Manager "optimized" on-screen; the way it was meant to be.*

Too many people make the Program Manager fill their screen; they don't leave room for the "open program" icons to show up along the bottom. It's too easy to lose track of programs and files if the Program Manager covers everything up.

PART TWO

Shortcuts

CHAPTER 4

Utilities

Utilities have a serious image problem. Let's face it—they're boring. People want fun, splashy *experiences* when they sit down at the computer. A program that sorts your file directory just can't compete with one that lets you fly over the San Francisco Bay bridge, shooting down enemy fighters along the way.

Many people don't know what utility programs do, never having used one (or simply not having known they were using one). Here's the scoop: Utilities don't help you do your work, they help do your computing.

Ever since using the first computer, people have clamored for improvements. For instance, when the same image or program menu appears on a monitor for a long time, the characters can "burn themselves in," leaving a ghost image.

You've probably seen "burn-in" on some older office computers that no one cares about. Wouldn't it be nice if there was a way to blank the screen without turning the monitor off? Sure. Somebody wrote a utility to accomplish the job.

Utilities are usually small programs that accomplish one task. For instance, DOS comes with several utility programs. DOS programs differ from DOS commands in that they're actual files saved on disk. (You won't find the COPY, DIR, or DEL commands anywhere on your DOS disk. Those commands come built into the COMMAND.COM program.)

Here's a quick rundown on some of the more useful utility programs that came bundled with your DOS disks. They're probably in the DOS directory of your hard drive.

CHKDSK.COM

When you run CHKDSK.COM, the screen looks something like this:

```
Volume PROGRAMS created Oct 9, 1989 4:44p
21344256 bytes total disk space
53248 bytes in 3 hidden files
102400 bytes in 47 directories
16439296 bytes in 801 user files
51200 bytes in bad sectors
4698112 bytes available on disk

655360 bytes total memory
595072 bytes free
```

SECRET: CHKDSK > FILE.TXT

How did I get the screen information from CHKDSK into this chapter without retyping it all by hand? I used something called "output redirection."

By typing CHKDSK > FILE.TXT, the CHKDSK program runs and sends all the information to FILE.TXT, so I can pull it into my word processor. The ">" character is a patrol boy of sorts, in that it moves traffic in a different direction. The ">" can be used with other DOS programs and commands, as well.

Check out these secrets, then fiddle with ">" on your own:

DIR > FILE.TXT Sends directory information to a file named FILE.TXT

DIR > PRN Sends directory information to the printer

DIR >> FILE.TXT Two ">>" symbols mean to add more information to the end of an already existing file.

You can send the output of many DOS commands and utilities into a text file by sticking the ">" character into the command line.

Utilities

This utility tells me I have 21,344,256 bytes (meaning 21,000K or 21 MB) of disk space on my hard drive, with 801 files stashed away in 47 different directories. CHKDSK also discovered the sneaky hidden files we talked about in Chapter Two.

The 51K of bad sectors means part of my hard drive is bad. No big deal, because I still have 21 MB of good hard drive space. That's a lot of space. Many hard drives have a few bad sectors on them (see Chapter 10).

I also have 4.6 MB of room left on my hard drive to add more programs. On its last two lines, CHKDSK says I have 655K of total RAM, with 595K available for programs. How do I have 655K of RAM when I'm only supposed to have 640K? Because I'm using the wonderful memory management utility, *QEMM*, that we discussed in Chapter One.

LABEL

This utility program lets you label your floppy disks. Not with a felt-tipped pen, but electrically. When you type DIR, the disk's label (known as VOLUME) scrolls across the screen:

```
Volume in drive B is PC SECRETS

Directory of B:\
BOOK.TXT 3184 8-07-91 2:36p
```

See? My floppy's called PC SECRETS. You can type "VOL" to see the disk's name, with no extraneous information.

To change the label on floppy B: to NEW NAME, I'd log to Drive B:, then type "LABEL NEW NAME". You can even name your hard drive TINA if you want. Aren't utilities fun?

MORE

This tiny program doesn't do anything by itself, but it's used with DOS commands mainly to view large files. When you type TYPE README.TXT, the file README.TXT will flow across your screen. If you're using a slow PC, you might be able to read it as the text flows by. But if you're using a '386, it will zip down the screen in a flash.

To view README.TXT one page at a time, type:

TYPE README.TXT |MORE

When the screen pauses with the words "— More —", press any key for the next page.

You can do the same thing with DIR on a huge directory by typing "DIR |MORE". You can do the same thing with less letters by typing "DIR /P". (This secret won't work with the "TYPE" command, though.)

SORT.EXE

Sort can be fun, but only with ASCII files. As the name implies, SORT will sort your lists alphabetically. Here are a few applications:

DIR |SORT

This will sort your directory as it appears on-screen. (for DOS 5.0, use DIR /O)

DIR |SORT |MORE

Same as above, but it will pause by screenfuls. (for DOS 5.0, use DIR /O |MORE

SORT < FILE.TXT

A sorted version of FILE.TXT will scroll across the screen.

SORT < FILE.TXT > FILESORT.TXT

This will take the contents of FILE.TXT, sort it, and save it in a file called FILESORT.TXT.

SORT works most predictably when you're dealing with ASCII files containing one-word lists, or one-line sentences.

Just about everybody has the utilities that we've discussed up until now. If you can't find them, dig out your MS-DOS disks (or PC-DOS or DR DOS) and look for 'em there.

Utilities 41

DOS Version 5

Doskey

The latest, greatest version of DOS adds a few more utilities. Doskey is one of the most welcome. It's a TSR (see Chapter One), meaning it loads, then hangs around in the background until called to action. As with other TSRs, it's best to put it in the AUTO-EXEC.BAT file so it will load automatically.

Doskey provides an easy way to repeat your last command line. For instance, let's say you wanted to switch to a subdirectory deep in the bowels of your hard drive. You'd type:

```
cd \PROJECTS\BOOKS\FICTION\BEAST
```

But if you made a small error, maybe typing BAEST instead of BEAST, DOS would freak out, saying "Invalid Directory."

With Doskey installed, you wouldn't have to retype the command until you got it right. You'd touch the <UpArrow> cursor key, and your misspelled command would pop up at the command line again. Backspace a few times to edit BAEST into BEAST, and hit <Enter>. Voila! Quick and easy!

Doskey can remember several of the past command lines, among many other things. Check the manual for details.

Dosshell

It's best to learn and remember as much about DOS commands as you can. But some people want the easy way out. They'll put yellow sticky notes all over their keyboard to remind them what to do.

The lazy way out is to use a shell program. DOS 5.0 comes with a DOS shell called—in the greatest tradition of RunningComputer-TermsTogether—Dosshell. The shell shows you a list of files on-screen; you perform DOS commands by simply pointing at the file name with the mouse and clicking.

It's much more comprehensive than the shell that came with DOS 4, if you ever checked that one out. If you have DOS 5.0, check out the shell program. Or just switch to *Windows*, like millions of other people.

> **SECRET: DOS 5.0 and EDIT**
>
> Here's a secret about the text editor included with DOS 5.0: It's not a text editor.
>
> Instead, it's a small program that runs over to the program QBASIC.EXE and borrows its editor. *QBasic* is a language allowing people to write their own programs. If you like EDIT but don't want to learn to program, don't save disk space by deleting QBASIC.EXE from your disk. If you do, EDIT won't work.

EDIT

Remember ASCII files, and how they're necessary for your CONFIG.SYS or batch files? Well, DOS 5.0 finally includes a small editor. It works very well compared to DOS's previous editor, a just-plain-dumb program called EDLIN.

SETVER

With so many different versions of DOS on the market, some programs become confused. If COOLPROG.EXE was written for DOS 3.3, for instance, the program may balk at loading under DOS 5.0. To solve this problem, use SETVER to trick COOLPROG.EXE into thinking it's using its favorite flavor of DOS. This line will make COOLPROG happy under DOS 5.0.

    SETVER COOLPROG.EXE 3.30

This command physically changes the SETVER.EXE file to reflect your desires. But since your computer only reads the SETVER file once (when it's booted up), you need to reboot your computer after using the command. That way the computer reads the updated version of SETVER when it starts up.

SETVER lets you revert to other versions of DOS, as well. Also,

Utilities

make sure you don't keep more than one copy of SETVER lying around, or your computer will be confused.

UNDELETE

Here's a welcome little utility. If you accidentally delete PRECIOUS.TXT, then type UNDELETE PRECIOUS.TXT, and your precious text file will magically reappear. You gotta use it right away, though, before you've created or changed any other files on your disk. Otherwise, your deleted file might have drifted too far away to be recovered.

To see which deleted files are still hanging around, type UNDELETE /list, and watch what turns up. You can even try this on your friends' computers to see what files they're trying to hide.

Other Utilities

DOS hasn't cornered the market on utilities; thousands of companies sell their own brands. For instance, a programmer named Peter Norton wrote a bunch of utilities, stuck 'em on a disk, and sold 'em under the fancy name, *Norton Utilities*. Many users call his work indispensable, even though he's always pictured wearing a pink shirt.

Other utilities, like *PC Tools*, work just like *Norton*'s. Here's what to expect from most of these commercial utilities:

Optimize/Defragment Your Hard Drive

Pretend your hard drive is an empty theater. When large groups arrive, they all sit together. The same thing happens when DOS copies a program to an empty hard drive—it puts all the program's code together.

But as the theater gets crowded, it's harder to find seats together, so groups arriving late have to break up, sitting where they can find room.

The same happens with your hard drive. After writing and erasing files from your hard drive, DOS has to scatter fragments of programs to wherever it can find room. It uses a FAT (File Allocation Table) to keep track of which seats (sectors) contain which files.

A defragmentation, or optimizing, program reads all the information on your hard drive, then writes it back to disk, lining up all the parts of a program next to the other parts. When your hard drive looks for a program, it will find all its parts in the same place, significantly speeding up operations.

It's a good idea to optimize your hard drive at least every other week, depending on how often you use your computer.

Disk Analysis Programs

Your hard drive is composed of bunches of sectors, where DOS stores program information. Every once in a while a sector can go bad, resulting in a loss of data. If it's a particularly important sector, DOS may lose the entire file.

Disk "doctors," or tools, let you examine your hard drive sector-by-sector, instead of file-by-file. You can search for key words in your data to see if lost information can be located. Once you've found it, you can write that sector to a disk file, then call that file into an editor to grab the information.

Colors, Cursors, Text Size

With utilities, you can decide what text size to display on your monitor. VGA monitors can display up to 50 lines per screen instead of the usual 25. Some people say that's too small to read. Other people like being able to see more of their document on-screen at the same time.

Similar utilities let you control the rate at which your cursor blinks, or whether it's a tiny underline or a solid block.

Public Domain

Since some utilities are so simple, their authors just give them away. These "free" programs are said to be released into the public domain, hence the name, "Public Domain" programs. Some of the best utilities are public domain.

Utilities

Other programmers give away their programs, but ask the users to send them a donation if they like their work and decide to use the program. These are called "shareware" programs. They're often just as good or better than the programs you'll find on the store shelves. But since the programmer didn't have enough money to pay for fancy packaging and distribution, he just gave the program away (hoping the program's users would feel guilty enough to send him a few bucks).

SECRET: Where to Find Utilities

Some companies make their living by selling public domain and shareware programs. They charge anywhere from two to six dollars per disk, and each disk contains one or more programs. Charging for free programs? Yep. The cost pays for the disk, the copying fees, postage, and packaging.

One of the biggest mail-order houses is called PC-SIG; it also publishes *Shareware Magazine*. The magazine contains articles, reviews, and lists of the latest shareware programs.

You could also try the bulk approach: EMS Professional Shareware Libraries bundles *all* the best shareware programs for a certain category, and sells the disks mail-order. For instance, its library of shareware programs for *Windows* contains more than 716 of the latest public domain and shareware programs: wallpaper, calendars, clocks, disk managers, telecom programs, screen drivers, games, graphics, icons, icon editors, and more.

The files come zipped onto more than 118 5¼-inch disks or about 31 3½-inch disks. The package includes a search program for locating programs by name, author, or text. At a cost of $149 for the bundle, that brings the individual program cost to about 21 cents each.

For more information, contact them at the following addresses:

PC-SIG, Inc.
1030D East Duane Avenue
Sunnyvale, CA 94086, USA

EMS
4505 Buckhurst Ct.
Olney, MD 20832, USA, (301) 924-3594

If you end up using a shareware program, it's better to mail in the small registration fee; if the program ever ends up on the shelves of software stores, it will cost a *lot* more.

Besides, the concept makes sense: It's better to try before you buy. That way, you can make sure the program *really* meets your needs before you have to start making payments on it.

Compression Utilities

Sooner or later, you'll have to deal with file compression. Just as you can squeeze a sponge and release it without causing damage, you can squeeze programs and data files to save disk space.

Various compression schemes grab a program, use a funky mathematical process to shrink it down, and then save it in this new, compressed format. Sometimes several files are squeezed together and saved under a single file name.

Several compression programs exist, but the most popular one is called ZIP. When a file has a ZIP extension, it's been "zipped" into a smaller format. You need the PKUNZIP program to "unzip" it before you can use it.

Many commercial programs UNZIP themselves as part of the installation process when they move from floppy disks to a space on your hard drive.

You can't run compressed programs; they must be decompressed first. Zipped files need the program PKUNZIP. Files with the ARC extension need the program UNARC, and programs ending in ARJ need the ARJ program.

If you're downloading programs from a computer BBS, look for the UNARC, ARJ, or PKUNZIP programs; you'll need to use them to decompress your files once they're on your hard drive.

Speaking of hard drives and compression, check out Chapter Ten for another compression technique.

CHAPTER 5

Keyboard Tricks and Tips

The tiniest detail about a keyboard can make or break a computer. Some keyboards feel too mushy; other keys take too much pressure to push down. Some make an annoying click; others have an <Enter> key that's too small.

Some people like their function keys across the top (where they can put sticky notes next to them); others like them along the side, making them easy to hit with their little finger.

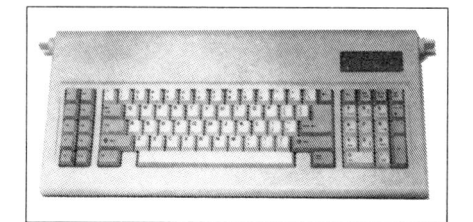

An 84-key keyboard with function keys along the side.

Enhanced 101-key keyboard with function keys along the top.

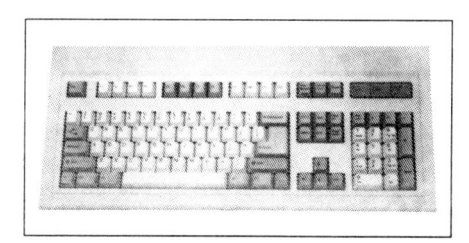

IBM's first PC, introduced in 1981, came with an 83-key keyboard; many people loved its feel. Unfortunately, the <Enter> key was a bit too small for easy reach. The <Shift> key was right next to the <PrtScn> key. Hundreds of innocent typists accidentally hit both at the same time, causing the computer to print the screen.

If the printer wasn't hooked up, the computer would freeze. You'd have to connect the printer, turn it on, and let the IBM dump its information. The <PrtScn> key only printed text, too. If you wanted to print any fancy graphics, you'd have to find another way.

It didn't have toggle lights, either, so you couldn't tell whether your <CapsLock> key was on or not. Same with the <NumLock> key.

IBM's next attempt, the AT keyboard, fixed a few of those flaws, and added an 84th key: <SysReq>. DOS doesn't use it. Neither do most people.

SECRET: XT, AT and You

When you finally upgrade from an XT to an AT, can you save some cash by reusing your old keyboard? Nope.

The AT keyboard is bidirectional; it not only sends signals to the computer, it receives them, as well. That's how the little green lights work above your enhanced keypad. If a software program automatically turns your <CapsLock> key on, for instance, the little green light will go on, too.

Even if your XT keyboard has lights, it's faking. It's just a keyboard switch, activated when you personally push the button. If your software turns the <CapsLock> key on, your XT's keyboard light won't turn on.

Since some of the key codes differ, as well, there's only one way to use your XT keyboard on an AT machine: Check underneath it for a small toggle switch. The better keyboards let you flip the switch to either an XT or AT layout, depending on your computer.

If you find an old keyboard as a garage sale bargain, look for the switch. Then check the cable. Some keyboards use different plugs. (And they call these computers "compatible"? Yeah, right.)

Keyboard Tips and Tricks

SECRET: What's Dvorak's Keyboard?

No, it's not the favorite keyboard of PC columnist John Dvorak. The name refers to a keyboard that's different from a standard typewriter.

The first typewriters brought problems. They were awkward, mechanical contraptions the size of pianos, and the keys tended to jam when somebody tried to type quickly. To slow the typists, the designers made the keyboard layout as awkward as possible.

They moved the most commonly used keys away from the "home row," where the typist's fingers normally rest on the keyboard. The typist's fingers had to move all over the keyboard to type, slowing them down so the keys wouldn't stick together.

Here's a secret: Another version of the story says the keyboard was laid out to make it easier for typewriter salesmen to demonstrate the machines: The letters required to spell "typewriter" are all on the top row, so the salesmen wouldn't have to look like "hunt-and-peck" bozos.

The traditional keyboard is called "qwerty," because that's the layout of the row of keys near the top left-hand corner.

By the 1930s, typewriters didn't have any more problems with key jams. A guy named August Dvorak, cousin of that classical music composer guy, designed a more efficient keyboard that lets the strong fingers of the right hand do most of the work. The vowels sit within easy reach on the home row. (By the way, the letters that spell "dvorak" don't appear next to each other, as do the letters that spell "qwerty.")

But it was too late. The world had seen a standard, forcing later products to remain compatible. Just as the personal computer's inefficient 640K RAM limit has haunted future computers, the typewriter's inefficient keyboard layout set the standard for all computer keyboards to come.

Of course, you could learn the dvorak layout, and you'd be fine on your computer at home. But when you deal with the other 99 percent of keyboards (at work, a friend's house, or a library), you'll be hunting and pecking.

Next down the line came the Enhanced keyboard. This monster holds 101 keys. It increased the number of function keys to 12, and moved them along the top. It added a numeric keypad along the right hand side, so people wouldn't have to hit the <NumLock> key and use the <Arrow> keys.

But IBM designers screwed up in a big way—they switched the position of the <Ctrl> and <Alt> keys. That's like swapping the gas and brake pedals on a car. Once you get used to something so basic, it's hard to break the habit.

The "corrected" 101-key layout put the <Ctrl> key back next to the <a> key, where it belongs. If you're stuck with the older keyboard, ask a computer guru friend for a copy of IBMFIX.COM, a small utility that swaps the <CapsLock> and <Ctrl> keys. (It doesn't swap the key caps, just the functions. Pry them off and move them yourself.)

Here's a secret: When buying a keyboard, check for "N-key" rollover. That means you can strike another key while the first one's held down repetitively. To check, hold down the <q> key until it repeats, then hit <w>, <e> and <r> one after the other. On a good keyboard, those letters should appear too. On a bad keyboard, the "q" will just hum right along, oblivious to the world.

Since a keyboard is such a personal thing, some programmers ended up writing utilities that customize the keys to their own liking. These utilities offer users a variety of choices: keys that can "click" or stay silent; the <NumLock> key can be on or off when the computer's first turned on. Or, the entire keyboard can be redefined: You can swap the <CapsLock> and <Ctrl> keys, for instance, so they're in a more familiar layout. You can even switch to Dvorak.

Other utilities expand the "keyboard buffer." When word processing, this means the computer stores your characters while it does something else, such as reading information off a floppy. When the computer comes back to attention, it will dump the contents of the buffer into the document, effectively "catching up" with your typing speed. Refer to Chapter Four, "Utilities," for information on how to grab these gems.

Keyboard Tips and Tricks 51

Macros

A utility that makes the <g> key do more than put a "g" on the screen is called a macro. At the risk of boring the reader by mentioning macro and utility in the same sentence, macros are one of the most powerful secrets of computing. They can be used at the DOS prompt, or from within any program.

Macros present a problem—namely, remembering what key does what. You can no longer rely on the single black letters on top of the keyboard.

Since computers work best when they're repeating things, macros work wonders inside programs. The better programs have them built in. You can install a macro in your word processor that will stick the current date at the top of the page, skip two lines, type your name and address, skip two more lines, and then type "Dear, " ready for you to begin your letter.

All of that information would appear on your screen when you use a macro. Macros are usually two-key sequences, like <Alt-E> or <Esc-L>. Whip out your program's manual, and check 'em out.

If your favorite program doesn't support macros, take heart: Utilities like Ashton Tate's *Control Room* let you assign macros as TSRs. They'll sit in the background, watching you press keys. When you hit the pre-defined macro sequence, *Control Room* will jump in and spit out the assigned macro characters.

Special Keys

The DOS keyboard contains a few keys not found on the typewriter. Here's the rundown on what they do. In this book, when the keys are enclosed in "< >", or "bracket" symbols, it means to hit those keys one after the other. To type <1> <2> <3>, you'd type the numeral 1, then 2, then three.

When the characters appear inside the brackets, next to each other (for example <Ctrl-G>), it means to hold down the <Ctrl> key while you hit the <G> key, then let go of both.

<Esc>

This key usually appears in an upper corner on your keyboard somewhere, and functions differently in different programs. For the most part, it lets you "escape," or stop whatever the computer or program happens to be doing. If you want a program to stop, first try pressing <Esc>. (This trick doesn't work with *WordPerfect*.)

<Ctrl>

By itself, this key doesn't do anything. It does, however, act like the <Shift> key on a typewriter: It adds meaning when pressed with another key.

<Ctrl-C>

Press this key combination to make the computer stop what it's doing (this command is often more powerful than <Esc>). It's sometimes called a "break" sequence. If you don't want it to work, open your CONFIG.SYS file and add the line "SET BREAK=OFF". This tells your computer not to stop and check for the "break" sequence, making it run faster. Of course, you can't use <Ctrl-C> anymore, though.

<Ctrl-S>

When you've typed TYPE README.TXT and the file scrolls across your screen too fast, type <Ctrl-S> to make it stop. Type <Ctrl-S> again, and the file will start to scroll again. When using a modem to talk with other computers, <Ctrl-S> works the same way, except you need to type <Ctrl-Q> to start things back up. See Chapter Nine for more details.

<Ctrl-G>

This sequence makes your computer beep, and it's handy to put at the end of batch files, so you know when your computer's through doing something. To use it, add the line "ECHO <Ctrl-G>" to your batch file. You can try it at the command line to hear what the beep sounds like.

Keyboard Tips and Tricks

<Ctrl-P>

While at the command line, this sequence "toggles" your printer on or off, so the text scrolling across your screen will head for the printer, as well. If your printer's not on, you'll get a nasty error message. Turn it on, then type <Ctrl-P>; type a line or two, then hit <Enter> to see it appear on the printer. Remember to turn it off by typing <Ctrl-P> again, for goodness sake. (Hitting <Ctrl-PrtScn> does the same thing.)

<NumLock>

Yep, it makes the arrow keys on the right side of your keyboard act like numbers.

<Ctrl-Alt-Del>

Hold down <Ctrl> and <Alt> and then hit the <Del> key to restart (reboot) your computer. Do this only as a last resort if your computer locks up, because when you reboot, you lose all the data you've added since the last time you saved your work.

<ScrollLock>

Just pretend it's not there. You don't need it. (It lets you choose between two cursor-key functions on some programs.)

<SysRq>

This key is for people who don't use DOS, so don't worry about it. Tell your coworkers it's a System Requisite key: It scans all codes typed at their keyboards and sends them to the Boss's office. And you'll be happy to disable it for only $10.

<CapsLock>

Just like on a typewriter, this key makes all the letters upper case. Unlike a typewriter's key, it doesn't stay hunkered down to remind you it's on; a little green light does that. And it doesn't affect the cursing !@#$%^&* keys along the top row, either. You still have to hit the <Shift> key to create those characters.

Function Keys

The typewriter keys weren't enough to perform all the funky computer commands, so the keyboard has function keys. They're often used in combination with other keys. For instance, pressing the <F7> key makes *WordPerfect* ask you if you want to leave the program. Pressing <Ctrl-F7> gives you a footnote.

But when at the DOS command line, the keys do something else, leading us to the big secret below.

SECRET: Repeat That Last Command, Sir

The first four function keys come in particularly handy at the DOS prompt. If you make a mistake typing a command, hit <F3>. The previously typed command will jump to the command line. Go ahead, try it!

The <F1> key does the same thing, but repeats the previous command one character at a time. The <F2> key is a little more sneaky.

Let's say you typed, "TYPE C:\AUTOEXEC.BAT" to see what's inside that file. Now, you want to see what's in your CONFIG.SYS file. The slow way would be to hit <F3> to have the previous command return, then hit the <Backspace> key to erase AUTO-EXEC.BAT, then type in CONFIG.SYS. Or you could hit the <F1> key five times to bring "TYPE C:\" back to the prompt, but that's tedious, too.

Instead, type <F2> and type the letter <a>. The <F2> key will retrieve the last command up to the letter "a," meaning it will instantly bring "TYPE C:\" to the command line, ready for you to add CONFIG.SYS, and be on your merry way.

It's not as exciting as DOS 5.0's Doskey utility, which remembers bunches of old commands. If you don't have DOS 5.0, look for the public domain utility, DosEdit, which works much like Doskey.

Keyboard Tips and Tricks 55

Keyboard Tricks

You don't have to use any "qwerty" keys at all to write a letter. DOS lets you enter any character using the <Alt> key and your numeric keypad. In fact, you *must* use this method to display some characters. Here's how it works:

The PC can display more than 255 characters on the screen. But only 127 of those characters can be displayed by directly typing on the keyboard. The rest of the characters are funny-looking graphic and mathematical symbols, as well as characters from foreign languages.

To enter these special characters, you must know the secret code, (it's listed in Appendix A). In the code chart, the character for the upper-case letter "T" is 84. Make a bet with a friend that you can type a "T" onto the screen without touching either the <t> or the <Shift> key. When you've bet a sizable chunk of real estate, hold down the <Alt> key, type 84 using the numeric keypad, then release the <Alt> key. The "T" will magically jump to the top of the screen.

There's not much point in typing three keys when you could have typed two. But sometimes you need to type characters that aren't on the keyboard. To make the infinity symbol, for instance, hold down <Alt>, type 236, and let go of the <Alt> key. The infinity symbol looks more like a pig's snout than infinity, but it's the closest you'll find in DOS.

Here are some phrases typed using the Alt-keypad trick:

Früstück (ü is 129)
¿Quién sabe? (é is 130, ¿ is 168)
ménage à trois (à is 133)
$\theta^2-\beta^2+\pi/n=?$ (look it up yourself)

Foreign Languages

To make things easier for computer users not living in the United States, DOS comes in international versions. Version 5.0 allows 24 different countries to customize DOS to their flavor. DOS usually comes preconfigured to the country where it's being sold.

It's relatively easy to accommodate foreign exchange students who want to write letters back home. To change your country setting under DOS 3.3 or later, look up the country table in the back of this book. For instance, to change to the Finland version, put this line in your CONFIG.SYS file. (Remember to reboot so the changes will take place.)

```
COUNTRY=358,C:\DOS\COUNTRY.SYS
```

Now the format for the time and date, currency, and foreign characters will show up the way they're supposed to in Finland. For instance, when you type "DIR" you'll see the dates listed in the format "09.15.91" instead of the usual American way.

To change the keyboard's layout to accommodate Finland's special characters, you'll have to add this command to your AUTOEXEC.BAT file:

```
KEYB SU,C:\DOS\KEYBOARD.SYS
```

Each new versions of DOS adds support for more countries. If your favorite country isn't included, it's time to upgrade.

ANSI.SYS

Here's a way to jazz up your computer's display. DOS comes with a method of adding colors to everything from your screen background and program menus to your DOS prompt. The secret is a file called ANSI.SYS, and it'll be on your DOS disk.

ANSI.SYS is called a "device driver." A device driver is a list of instructions that tell DOS how to deal with a piece of software. You'll see device drivers for your monitor, sound cards, special memory management software, and other computing goodies. You'll recognize them because they all use the extension "SYS".

Most programs don't use ANSI.SYS; they deal with your PC's hardware directly, bypassing DOS's built-in screen codes. But to check it out, add this line to your CONFIG.SYS file:

```
DEVICE =C:\DOS\ANSI.SYS
```

Keyboard Tips and Tricks

We're assuming you've copied the ANSI.SYS file to your DOS directory. Also, remember to reboot your computer after you've changed your CONFIG.SYS file, because DOS only reads that file once, when it boots up.

You can't type ANSI codes directly; that would be too easy. Instead, you have to stick them into one of three formats: a text file to be TYPEd, a batch file to be executed, or your DOS prompt.

Once you've entered the commands, you can change the color of your text and background, move the cursor around the display, erase a line of text, or clear the entire screen and perform other cool tricks.

ANSI codes depend on the "Esc" character, which brings a problem: When you hit the <Esc> key, the program doesn't print the "Esc" character; it thinks the <Esc> is part of its own commands.

Therefore, you can't enter the commands at the command line,

SECRET: The Menu Maker

ANSI codes can create a decorative front-end menu, like this:

M E N U
Choose the number of the program you want to run:

1) Word Processor
2) Spreadsheet
3) Game

Each of the lines in the menu can be a different color by sprinkling ANSI codes in with the text. Name the file MENU.TXT, and put these two lines at the end of your AUTOEXEC.BAT file:

CLS
TYPE MENU.TXT

Then write a batch file named 1.BAT that loads up your word processor; 2.BAT will load your spreadsheet, and 3.BAT will run a game. At the end of each of these three batch files, make them type MENU.TXT. Be sure to put all those batch files on your path.

You've just saved the cost of a front-end menu, and best of all, you can customize it yourself.

because <Esc> cancels what you've typed. So, we'll try the easiest way of introducing the Esc character: embedding it within the DOS prompt itself. If you remember the "prompt" chapter, you learned that $e stands for the Esc character. We'll use it now.

At the command line, type:

PROMPT = $e[1;32;45m$p$g

With a color monitor, that command will give your monitor green letters on a purple background. Here's the rundown:

$e = the necessary escape command
[= the trigger that works with $e
1 = high intensity text
32 = green text in the foreground
45 = purple, or magenta in the background
m = the closing symbol for the color sequence
$p = current directory
$g = greater than sign

The semicolons space out the three numbers that order the colors. Here's the formula:

[n;nm where n is the attribute and "m" is the closing symbol.

n Value	Color	Monochrome
0	normal	normal
1	high intensity	high intensity
2	normal intensity	normal intensity
4	blue	underline
5	blinking	blinking
7	inverse video	inverse video
8	invisible	invisible

Keyboard Tips and Tricks

Color	Foreground	Background
Black	30	40
Red	31	41
Green	32	42
Yellow	33	43
Blue	34	44
Magenta	35	45
Cyan	36	46
White	37	47

Instead of embedding ANSI codes in the prompt, it's sometimes better to put them in a text file, and then use the TYPE command to bring them to the screen.

PART THREE

Hardware Hints

CHAPTER 6

Monitors

Let's get to the heart of the question right now. Which monitor is better: black and white (known as monochrome), or color?

Everybody secretly wants color, but they need a way to rationalize the higher price. So we'll start off with a monitor secret: Buy the color monitor, and not just because it looks good for games. Color will make *all* of your programs work better, and for several reasons.

Today, even Serious Business Programs rely on color to make them easier to use. It's easier to differentiate between menus, for instance, if they're displayed in different colors. Also, if your cursor is a contrasting color, it's easier to spot in a sea of text.

Furthermore, since most of today's programmers design their programs to use color, the programs usually look terrible in monochrome. The screen's too busy, and it's difficult to tell what's highlighted and what's not. Owners of inexpensive laptops face this problem every day. Just ask 'em.

People used to say monochrome monitors worked better for text or word processing. Not anymore. Today's VGA monitors have just as good or better resolution as the black and whites. (Or, to be more precise, the amber and greens found on most monochrome monitors.)

Color Choices

In the old days of computing, people hooked their computers to their television sets. Because of its low resolution, the TV screen couldn't show more than 40 characters on a single line. Plus, the letters looked fuzzy.

Today, you'll find plenty of color monitors on the market, all of which will out-perform your TV. Your purchase decision shouldn't be that difficult, once you understand the abbreviations. Here's a rundown on today's color monitors:

CGA (Color Graphics Adapter)

The CGA monitors, IBM's first attempt at color, failed miserably. They look terrible for text, and the colors are awful. CGA monitors can only display four colors on-screen at the same time. Avoid these monitors under all circumstances.

EGA (Extended Graphics Adapter)

EGA monitors, the industry's second shot at color, worked well. The text is clearly defined, and up to 16 colors can appear on-screen at the same time. To save some money, scan the classifieds for somebody selling an old EGA monitor. Most people who originally bought EGA have now moved up to VGA. EGA isn't really all that bad, although it's fading fast.

VGA (Video Graphics Array)

VGA monitors are stunning, compared to the other two. They can show 256 colors on-screen at once, leading to photographic-quality images. (It's photo quality if you squint or step back a few feet.) Unfortunately, VGA can only display those 256 colors at a low, chunky resolution.

S-VGA (Super VGA)

The well-defined industry standards stopped at VGA, but the manufacturers kept on going. The super VGA cards will produce the same 256 colors on-screen at the same time as VGA, but with much higher resolution. Some of the newer cards can display thousands of colors simultaneously. Unfortunately, S-VGA cards made by different manufacturers work differently, so you'll probably have to tell your programs exactly what brand of card and monitor you're using.

Monitor Facts

Monitors don't work by themselves; they need cards to tell them what to display. The cards slide inside your computer, leaving just a plug showing. That's where you plug in your monitor's cable. Since the cards and monitors depend on each other, you need to buy a VGA card when you buy your VGA monitor. The older EGA cards can't handle VGA graphics.

Sometimes you'll get lucky, and be able to merely upgrade your card instead of buying a new one. For instance, if you move up from VGA to S-VGA, you can sometimes just add some memory to your

---

SECRET: Monitoring Your Health

Is it bad for you to stare at a computer monitor all day?

Nobody has the definitive answer, unfortunately. Some studies say VDTs (health officials like to call monitors "video display terminals") can emit harmful radiation. Other studies say, "Rubbish, they're safer than a bowl of oatmeal."

The controversy started in 1968 when Congress grew concerned about children who sat too close to their teievision sets. Congress passed an act requiring all commercial appliances to limit their x-radiation (x-rays) to minuscule levels. The x-ray situation has improved, but monitors still release small levels of electromagnetic radiation.

Currently, our government is satisfied that computer monitors are safe. Still, keep the brightness turned down. That'll save wear and tear on your eyes, as well as the monitor. And take a break to stretch your legs and let your eyes focus on something else for a while. . . . It can't hurt.

> **SECRET: Amber or Green?**
>
> Which monochrome monitor is easier to read, amber or green? It depends on who you talk to. Some health studies say amber is better for the eyes. Other health studies say green works better for people with astigmatism. Take a look at both types before making your decision. Or, sidestep the decision altogether and just buy a color monitor. You'll feel better each time you use it.

VGA card. Most VGA cards have 256K of RAM, whereas S-VGA cards need 512K or more to show all their pretty colors at once.

Still undecided about what monitor to buy? Go for the VGA monitor—you won't be disappointed. The industry's heading in that direction, and most programmers design their software for VGA. If you can afford a super VGA card, go ahead, but make sure you're buying from a well-established video company, one that software makers will want to support.

Define Your Monitor Terms

The number of colors a monitor can display provides a good gauge as to quality, but watch out for a few more terms.

Pixels: Monitors work when electrons make bits of phosphor glow along their screens. Each little glow spot is a pixel (picture element). The more pixels, the better the complete picture will look.

Resolution: This determines how many pixels a monitor can display. The pixels line up in rows and columns like Post Office boxes. VGA monitors line up their pixels in rows of 640 by 480. Increased resolution means more pixels, which means a better picture. Some super VGA monitors can display images with 1024 by 768 resolution.

Dot Pitch: Monitors display color by flashing red, green and blue spots in varying intensities. Like mixing finger paints, the spots create different shades of colors. If the three spots are very close together, they'll create a better picture. The closer they are, the smaller the dot pitch. Look for a dot pitch of at least 0.28 millimeter.

Monitors 67

Trouble-Shooting

When you first turn on your computer and hear it whir to life, you should see some messages flash across the top of your screen. If you don't, something's wrong.

First, check the monitor's knobs. This may sound dumb, but is it turned on? Also, somebody might have turned the brightness down all the way to fool you. Or, since the knobs turn easily, you might have accidentally turned them yourself by rubbing against them when reaching for a floppy disk.

Next, check the cords. Most monitors have two cords, one for power, and the other to grab the picture information from the CPU. Check the power cord first, making sure it hasn't pulled from the wall. Then wiggle the cord where it connects to the monitor. Finally, wiggle the cord where it plugs into the video card in the back of your computer.

If either of the connections has loosened, consider buying a tiny screwdriver; most of the cords contain tiny screws for more secure fastening.

Screen Savers

Take a look at some old monochrome monitors in an office someday. If they've been displaying the same program for years,

---

SECRET: Be Careful With That Screwdriver, Eugene.

Feel free to fiddle with your monitor's contrast knobs. If you're feeling particularly adventurous, grab a small plastic screwdriver to adjust the alignment.

But don't ever open your monitor and fiddle with the insides. To display pictures, monitors spray electrons from the back of the monitor to the back of the screen. These "electron guns" use thousands of volts of electricity, and they'll do much more than give you rock and roll hair.

Taking it apart won't do you any good, anyway. There's nothing in there you can fix by yourself.

you'll know. By looking at the faint image that's been "burned" into the screen, you'll be able to tell what program's been running.

When the monitor fires its electron guns at the phosphor, the phosphor glows. But if certain parts glow more than others, they'll wear out sooner. That's why these monitors need a "screen saver" program. A screen saver loads itself into your computer's RAM when you first turn it on. The program then watches while you type. When you haven't typed anything for a while, it assumes you've left and don't need the monitor anymore. So it turns the screen blank.

Most screen savers let you adjust the amount of time before they'll blank your screen; about four minutes seems adequate.

EGA and VGA monitors usually don't have a problem with

SECRET: Hot Stuff

Don't run your monitor any brighter than necessary. Find the brightness control right off the bat, and adjust the picture until it looks comfortable for your eyes.

Electrons from the monitor's electron gun strike a phosphor coating on the inside of the screen, causing the phosphor to glow. Like everything else, phosphor eventually wears out.

So don't glow brighter than necessary. Try positioning the monitor so there's no glare from an open window. That way the two light sources won't have to compete with each other.

Need something to cut the glare, but don't want to spend the money on an officially sanctioned "Glare Filter" from a computer store? Then make one from a pair of panty hose or stockings: Cut off one leg, then cut off the foot. Make a lengthwise cut down the remaining tube, then stretch it over the front of your monitor. Hold it in place with a rubber band or tape.

Believe it or not, the tiny holes in the panty hose will act like the tiny holes in a glare filter, often making it easier to read the screen. Skip the lace ones, however, and don't let the seams get in the way.

And if you use this makeshift screen at work, your computer will look so pathetic that your boss will probably take pity on you and buy you the real thing!

burn-in because of their better resolution and physical structure. Still, some people worry about burn-in. And if you're going to be running the same program over and over, you should consider a screen saver anyway, no matter what kind of monitor you're using.

Screen savers are bundled with some monitors. Others can be purchased at software stores. Instead of blanking the screen, some screen savers fill it with pictures of moving fish, jumping kaleidoscopes, or other images that keep the same pixels from burning a constant image into the monitor's phosphor.

Line Size

With the increased resolution of EGA and VGA monitors comes another trick: more lines on the screen. If you're working on a long document and want to see more of it on-screen at the same time, switch "video line" modes.

For instance, monitors usually display 25 lines at a time on the screen. An EGA monitor can display 43 lines at a time, giving you more to work with. VGA monitors can display even more lines simultaneously. Unfortunately, increased amounts of lines lead to smaller letters.

Experiment with the utilities that came with your color monitor. Lost them? Well, some programs allow you to change the display's line size as a menu option. It's worth checking out.

CHAPTER 7

Printers

Some people can squeak by without a color monitor, or without buying a hard drive. But just about everybody needs a printer. Eventually you'll need to document the results of your work, or show it to somebody else for comment.

The end result of most computing work is to reproduce your efforts on paper. Several printers on the market can imitate what's on your screen, all with differing results.

The best printers make your letters look as if they were typed out by hand. Strangely enough, it's still a stigma for many businesses to admit they use computers for their correspondence.

Here's a look at printers on the market and their best uses.

Dot Matrix Printers

These printers work by firing tiny pins against an ink-soaked ribbon, which presses against the paper, leaving tiny ink spots. The more pins, the more spots, and the better quality the final image will be. Printers using 24 pins will look better (and cost more) than the older technology of 9-pin printers. The printed quality of these printers comes very close to resembling typewritten output, so they are referred to as "Near Letter Quality" (NLQ) printers.

Advantages: These printers can be quick in low-resolution mode, so they're great for printing rough drafts. They're versatile, because they can print graphics as well as text. They're inexpensive, too.

Disadvantages: The printers can be somewhat noisy for an office setting.

Secrets: Just draping a handkerchief over these boys can quiet 'em down. If you have the money, you can buy a specially soundproofed box to put them in.

When changing the settings on these, for example from draft quality to near letter quality, you usually have to turn the printer off, and then turn it on again. It only reads its instructions once, when it's set up, so it won't know if you've changed something.

When you print a document from your favorite word processor, check to see how far over the printer head slides before it starts printing. When you've identified the margin, use some White-Out

---

SECRET: Double-Duty WD-40

When your dot matrix printer doesn't seem to be printing as dark as it used to, it might be time for a new ribbon. Or maybe not, if you try out this secret. Sometimes the ribbon's just dried out, and it can be rejuvenated.

Remove the old cartridge, and carefully pry open the plastic top. Use a small screwdriver and lift up slowly and evenly all around the edges; eventually, it will pop off. Set the cartridge down on several large pieces of newspaper. (This could get a little bit messy.)

You'll see the ribbon coiled up inside the cartridge. Slowly spray all parts of the ribbon with WD-40. Don't soak the ribbon, but coat all parts of it evenly. Then, set it aside for several days, letting the WD-40 seep into the fibers.

Put the lid back on, and pop it in your printer. If the ribbon's too dark, and you see streaking, let it dry out a few more days, and try again. (Store any other ribbons in sealed plastic bags to keep them from evaporating more than necessary.)

The ribbon's cloth will eventually wear out, but you'll be able to reuse it three or four times.

or a small piece of tape to market that spot on your printer's ruler bar. That makes it easier to line up the paper with where your printer's going to be printing.

Impact Printers

Known as Daisy Wheel or Thimble printers, these function much as a typewriter. They push the outline of an individual character against a ribbon, leaving the character's image on the paper.

Advantages: Since their output is indistinguishable from a typewriter, they're known as Letter Quality printers.

Disadvantages: They're very slow, very noisy, and they can't print any graphics. To print foreign characters or use different fonts, you need to purchase special attachments. For these reasons, they're on their way out. Pass them up unless you find a bargain.

Secrets: Many businesses are now replacing these with laser printers. I bought an old impact printer for $15. It's great for printing addresses on envelopes. Check thrift stores and office supply stores for closeouts on the "wheels" or "heads" these printers use. Different wheels contain different fonts, and it's nice to have a variety.

If you use an impact printer a lot, definitely buy an enclosed cover to quiet the thing down.

Inkjet Printers

Relative newcomers in the marketplace, they work like dot matrix printers except that they squirt the ink directly onto the page. You'll find the same little dots.

Advantages: They're very quiet, usually smaller, and often just as fast as other printers. The higher-end inkjets work with color.

Disadvantages: Since they're relatively new, first make sure your prime software packages will support them.

Secrets: Although inkjet printers will work with a wide variety of paper, you'll find different quality output with each. Since the printer is squirting ink, the ink tends to bleed into the paper, producing fuzzy output. Also, the ink can smear before it has a chance to dry, especially with earlier printer models.

Special inkjet paper is coated: Make sure you print on the correct (coated) side. Which side is coated? Grip a stack of paper by the sides, hold it horizontally, and see how far it flops. Turn it over, and compare the dangles. The side that curves down the most is the proper side to print on; put this side face-down in Epson's DeskJet.

To be safe, print a couple of sample sheets whenever you're trying a new paper type. See which side prints best, then store the unused paper the proper way so you just grab it and stuff it into the printer.

> **SECRET: Inputting the Output**
>
> Sometimes it's handy to print out a listing of all the files on a disk or directory. Here's a quick method that works with most printers. Try it out and see if it works for yours:
>
> Type "DIR > LPT1" and press <Enter>. Instead of appearing on your monitor, the output will head for your printer.

Thermal Printers

These heat up special paper to form characters.

Advantages: They're small, lightweight, and often battery powered.

Disadvantages: They lack good resolution. Also, the special paper is expensive, leading to limited applications (for instance, fax machines).

Secrets: It's no secret that these portable printers work well with laptops. Bring an extra set of batteries, and an extra roll of paper, so you don't run out at an inopportune time.

Laser Printers

The Cadillac of printers, laser printers work much like copy machines. They grab toner off a rotating metal drum, dab it onto the page in the correct areas, then fuse it to the paper using heat and pressure.

Printers

Advantages: These printers provide excellent quality with text or graphics. The output looks almost as good as a newspaper page.

Disadvantages: They're expensive, costing more than $600 (although knowing computers, the price will probably drop by the time you read this). Also, replacement toner cartridges can be expensive.

Secrets: Want that newsletter to look nice but you can't justify the cost of a laser printer? Check the yellow pages: You can usually rent a printer either by the hour (best) or by the page (worst, since it usually takes two pages of rejects before one turns out OK).

Tired of spending money on new toner cartridges every two months? Then recycle your old ones. Again, check the yellow pages for printers or recyclers. Or ask your dealer. Chances are, you can cut your toner costs by one third or more.

Does your printer smell funny? Every 30,000 pages, it's smart to replace your printer's "ozone" filter. These filters remove the polluting gas before it escapes the printer. Check the manual; sometimes you can snap out the old one and pop in a new one. Other times you must take it to the dealer.

If you're printing a resume, or any other document that should look top notch, make your laser printer print four completely black pages, one after the other. (Use a paint or graphics program to create

---

SECRET: What's PostScript?

A company named Adobe developed a way for computers and printers to talk to each other; the result, a language called PostScript, has become a standard. The language defines how your printer depicts letters and shapes. Since it's a standard, PostScript-capable printers will all print the same text the same way.

They're slow; PostScript printers contain a computer inside them to interpret your computer's commands. And they're expensive, adding about $1,000 to the cost of the printer. But if you're seriously considering graphics work, buy a PostScript-compatible printer.

a file of pure black.) This will distribute the toner evenly on the drum, making the next copy look particularly pristine.

Print Spoolers

Your computer can work much faster than any printer. In fact, a printer can be the bottleneck for many computing chores. When printing information, your computer must sit still, sending line after line to the printer. Meanwhile, the user twiddles his thumbs.

Luckily, DOS comes with a "print spooler," known simply as PRINT.COM. You'll find it on the disks that came with your copy of MS-DOS. PRINT lets you print the file in the background while you're working on another file.

To print the file "FOOD" for instance, type "PRINT FOOD" at the DOS prompt, and hit return. DOS will toss it to the printer.

If you want to insert printer formatting, check your software's printing command, and have it print the file to disk rather than to the

---

SECRET: Back to the Typewriter

Want to jot down a quick shopping list, but you don't have pencil and paper handy? Turn on your printer, and try this trick:

At the DOS prompt, type:

COPY CON PRN

And then press <Enter>. Start typing your list; each time you hit <Enter> at the end of a line, the words will appear on your printer. To eject the page, hold down the <Ctrl> key and press <L>. You'll see the character ^L appear on your screen; the caret in front of the L stands for the <Ctrl> key. When you're through, and want to return to your regular computing, hold down the <Ctrl> key and press <Z>. That's it!

If you have a pencil but no paper, you can make your printer spit out a sheet by typing this at the DOS prompt:

ECHO ^L > PRN

You can try this "page ejection" trick when you have a half-printed page "stuck" in a laser printer.

Printers

printer. Then use the DOS PRINT command to print that file, which will include printer formatting commands.

If you have a RAM drive (see Chapter One), you can copy the whole operation over there for faster execution.

One last thing: Consider buying a "power director." It's a box with a bunch of switches that usually rests underneath your monitor. You plug all your peripherals into it, and then use the box's switches to turn your monitor, computer and printer on and off. It can save you a lot of groping.

Also, you can turn the printer on only when you need it, saving electricity. Unfortunately, printers consume electricity even when they're not printing.

CHAPTER 8

Expansion Boards

IBM manufactured only the keyboard on its first PC. Everything else came from other manufacturer's parts. That concept hasn't changed much over the years. Today, the IBM-compatible PC is still a collection of different manufacturer's parts working together as one unit.

Since it's relatively easy to add and subtract parts, owners can tinker with their IBM-compatible computers, adding new toys, trying different brands of components, and customizing the machines to fit their specific needs.

This innovative concept, known as "open architecture," sparked high sales. Apple, on the other hand, kept its later systems closed: Macintosh users must buy most of their spare parts from Apple, and the Macintosh add-ons usually cost more than if they'd been made by a competitor.

The open system made the IBM PC an attractive computer, and the marketing strategy worked, sort of. Today, more people own IBM-compatible computers than any other type. (People don't own very many of IBM's own brand of computer, but that's another story.)

When you buy an IBM-compatible computer, the dealer expects you to return for more goodies. There's plenty of room: Inside each

> **SECRET: IBM, MCA, and You**
>
> The phrase "IBM compatible" became complicated several years ago when IBM brought out its Personal System family of computers (PS/1, PS/2). IBM created a worldwide standard with its XT and AT computers. But since IBM used open architecture, other companies released their own, cheaper compatible computers.
>
> More people bought the less-expensive computers than IBM's computers. So IBM changed design slightly, using a different "expansion bus" (tech-talk for the row of slots inside your computer where you can plug in cards). This new "standard" hasn't caught on very well.
>
> If you bought an IBM PS/1 or PS/2, you can't use the regular plug-in cards that everybody else uses. You must use a special MCA (Micro Channel Architecture) version of the card. It can add up to $100 onto the price of the card.
>
> Be forewarned.

computer, you'll find five or eight "slots," depending on your model. (These slots are known as the "expansion bus.") They serve as parking spaces for peripherals, known as "cards," "boards," or simply, "goodies." These cards, when slid into the slots, give your computer extra abilities.

By sliding in a sound card, for instance, your computer can play a stereo soundtrack with games. Special memory cards let your computer run more powerful software. And fax cards let your computer send and receive faxes like a fax machine.

You can see the ends of the cards by looking at the back of your PC. See all those wires and cables? With the exception of the power cord and the keyboard cable, all of those wires and cables are plugging into the ends of cards.

Installing a Card

Cards aren't difficult to install and replace, if you work step by step. First, grab a pencil and paper to take notes. If you're going to

Expansion Boards **81**

be moving dip switches (a plastic row of tiny on/off switches), sketch their positions on paper. You might even want to make a photocopy of the board before you install it, so you can see all the settings. (If you have a Polaroid "Instant" camera, now's your chance to use it!)

Next, take precautions against static electricity. That little snap, crackle you hear when petting a cat could be enough to kill your computer. Discharge any built-up static electricity by touching your computer's case before working on any of its internal components. And don't shuffle around on the carpet while you work, either.

SECRET: It's Got a Screw Loose

Here's a secret when taking the case off your computer. You'll see the screws on the back of your computer, but which screws do you remove? Not all of them.

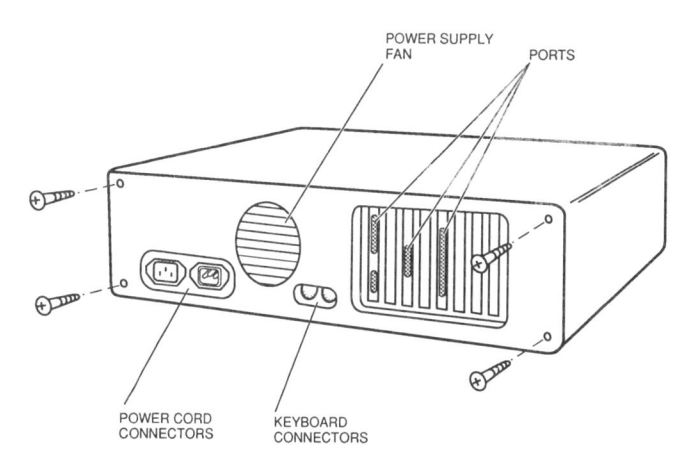

[Illustration of computer back panel with labels: POWER SUPPLY FAN, PORTS, POWER CORD CONNECTORS, KEYBOARD CONNECTORS]

Just take off the four screws around the perimeter of the back edge. The other ones, the ones surrounding the fan, are holding on your power supply. Leave them be.

And be sure to put the screws in a safe place, where they won't roll off the table and hide in the carpet when you're trying to put them back in.

Third, gather your tools. You'll need two small screwdrivers, (regular and Phillips), a paper-clip or pencil to flip dip switches, and a vacuum cleaner. Those tiny, battery-powered automobile vacuums work well to suck dust from the insides of your computer.

Now, read the directions that came with the card. Sometimes you'll need to flip a switch or move a jumper before installing it. If you wait until you've already installed the card, it's very difficult to change any of the switches, causing you much aggravation.

When digging inside your computer, play it safe. Before taking the cover off your PC, turn the thing off and unplug it. Then remove the cover, and set it to one side. You'll see the cards and slots immediately, as they run lengthwise from back to front.

Find a slot that's not being used, and look to see if it has a "cover." That's the small silver piece of metal that blocks the hole from the back.

There's a single screw holding down that cover. Remove the screw, and the cover will come off. Save the screw; throw away the cover. Unless you remove the card, you'll never need that cover again.

Now, position your new card over the slot. The flat, silver side of the card points to the rear, and the "plug" end faces down. Rock the card back and forth until the plug begins to slide into the slot, then give it a good push until it's seated firmly.

Now, grab the screw that held on the cover, and put it in the same hole, bolting down the card in the process. That's about it. Put the case back on, attach any required cables, plug the computer back in, and it should recognize the new card when you turn it on.

Types of Cards

When you buy a computer, it should come with several cards already installed: a video card and an I/O (Input/Output) card. The I/O card will probably contain a serial port (also known as a COM port), a parallel port (sometimes known as a printer port), and, if you're lucky, a game port to plug in the joystick.

Those are the bare bones; the next few cards will help add some

Expansion Boards 83

flesh to your computing. Also, even after you've added the cards, you're not through. All the cards require software, usually referred to as "drivers" to take advantage of their features. Some cards require a few other gizmos, as you'll see.

Which Slot, Jack?

When faced with a choice of slots, which one should you use? Here's a secret: It really doesn't matter. Almost. The '286 and '386 computers have one slot that's bigger than the standard size. If you

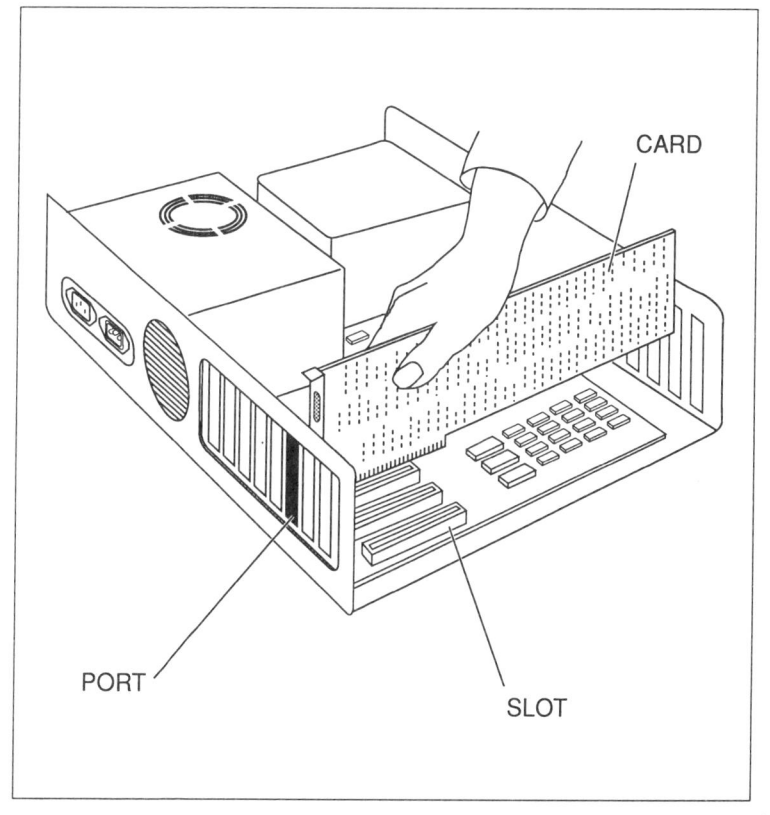

When you push the card into a slot, the card's ports show from the back of the computer. Be sure you've turned off the power first.

> **SECRET: A Slice of Slots**
>
> Since you only have a limited number of slots, what do you do when you run out, but still want to install another goodie? Look for a card that combines several functions on one card. For instance, older computers used a separate card for a serial port, a game port, and the clock.
>
> Find a newer card that contains all these capacities, and you've freed up two slots. No room for a sound card? Check out ATI's AudioFX card. It combines a sound card with a VGA graphics card, freeing up a slot.
>
> Also, you don't need a separate card with two game ports in order to use two joysticks at the same time. Many computer stores sell "Y" adapters for joysticks. You plug the base of the "Y" into the single port, and use the two arms, one for each joystick. It works just as well as having two separate game ports.
>
> You might want to upgrade: Most newer computers come with a serial port built right into the motherboard, saving a slot.
>
> Keep your eyes open for innovative combinations to meet your particular needs.

have a big card, put it in the bigger slot. (Big cards, especially graphics cards, will often work in small slots, but not as quickly.)

Otherwise, just put your card in the slot where it fits best. Sometimes you'll have to rearrange the cards so they mesh: Some have lots of wires on one side, which can rub against other bulky cards. It can be like a jigsaw puzzle, but eventually, everything should fit.

Sound Cards

A wide variety of companies sell sound cards that let your computer play and record music and sounds. I like the Pro Audio Spectrum card: It can record or play any sounds in high-quality stereo. It can play back any music recorded using the "Adlib" music standard (found in most games and some presentation packages). It even contains a game port for your joystick.

Expansion Boards

Finally, it contains a MIDI port, so you can hook up a keyboard or synthesizer to your computer and record and play back music.

All of these sound cards require a pair of speakers so you can hear them. You'll also need a microphone for recording. Some let you use the typing keyboard as a piano, but you'll be better off with a "real" musical keyboard. Some require an amplifier, too, so you can hear the sounds. And if you install more than one sound card (one for music, the other for voices and sound effects, known as a Digital Audio Channel), you'll need an audio mixer to hear them at the same time.

Fax/Modems

We'll be discussing these in detail in the next chapter. Essentially, they turn your computer into a fax machine; a modem lets your computer exchange data with other computers.

Both faxes and modems require a phone cord to be run from the card to the wall; some let you plug a phone extension into the back of the card, too, so it's easy to keep a phone on your desk. Also, to send any pictures, you'll need a scanner.

Scanner

Scanners slide over newspapers and magazines to copy their images into your computer. They plug into a card, which sits in your computer. They're slow on an XT, but reasonably fast on a '386. The graphics files they create are usually huge.

Also, scanners can grab text, but usually your computer won't

---

SECRET: Problems?

A card might not work for several reasons, but if it just recently started acting up, here's a secret: Try removing it and rubbing a pencil eraser along the connections where the card fits into the slot. This can remove dirt that might be causing a bad connection. Sometimes it's a cheap fix.

be able to read it as separate words or characters. It will keep the text as a graphics file, suitable only for graphics programs.

Some of the newer scanners, however, come with Optical Character Recognition software (OCR). With OCR, scanners can convert some text into actual text characters, recognizing more than 90 percent of the letters and numbers. Be sure to proofread carefully to avoid embarrassing mistakes.

Memory Cards

These cards contain memory chips. Sometimes older computers can't fit any more RAM onto the motherboard, so companies will stick RAM onto a card, ready to be slipped into a slot.

Since this type of RAM is known as expanded memory (see Chapter One), you'll need to stick an expanded memory driver into your CONFIG.SYS file so the computer can use it.

Video Cards

You read about these in an earlier chapter, so here's just one tip: You can buy a card that's better than your monitor. For instance, if you have an older VGA monitor that can only display 640 by 480 resolution, you can still use a super VGA card that's capable of 1024 by 768 resolution. Your monitor won't be able to display that high of resolution, but it *will* be able to display additional colors.

Port Conflicts

Whenever you install a card, it's like sticking something into one of your computer's mouths. Unfortunately, the computer has a limited number of mouths. That's why you need to learn about "addresses" and "interrupts."

Cards that let the computer send or receive data need a proper address and an interrupt. Cards send data "In" and "Out"; to keep track of all the data as it flows, the computer uses an "I/O address map." Each card needs a separate address on that map to function properly.

Expansion Boards

Cards also need an interrupt so the computer will listen to them. They need to be able to stop the computer and make it do something else. When you click a button on a mouse, for instance, it sends an interrupt request (IRQ) to your computer. Your computer then stops, and heads in the new direction, as specified by the mouse's location on the screen when the click occurred.

The problem comes when two cards try to use the same address or interrupt, confusing the computer in the process. Modems and sound cards are notorious for this. To avoid the problem, try to keep track of what cards are using each address and interrupt; then choose spare ones for your new cards. Write down the addresses and interrupt for each new card. Sometimes your software will ask for the information.

You set the interrupts and addresses on the card by flicking its switches or moving its jumpers. If you're lucky, you'll get it right the first time.

If you're not, keep trying different settings until you find one that works. This can be terribly time-consuming, especially when the card has its jumpers and switches mounted near the bottom: You must physically remove the card, try a different setting, reinsert it, and turn your computer back on.

PART FOUR

Fun and Finesse

CHAPTER 9

Modem Magic

Ray wanted to go fishing, but he wasn't sure what the weather would be like. He turned on his modem, and in less than a minute, a current weather map appeared on his computer's monitor.

Tracy heard from a friend that an earthquake had just struck a city where some of her friends live. She turned on her modem, and soon she was reading Associated Press news reports about the quake and its damage.

Jonathan received a confusing error message on his computer's monitor. He turned on his modem, called an "electronic bulletin board," and posted a note about his dilemma. When he called back later that afternoon, he found several people had posted solutions to his problem.

The key word here is "modem." It's a computer gizmo that costs about $100 and connects your computer to your telephone line. Once it's connected, you use software to tell your computer to dial up other modems, which are also connected to computers.

And that's where the fun begins. With a modem, you have access to more information than you'll ever find in a library. You can get personalized responses to thousands of subjects; you can find free software. You can play games against other people.

But first, you have to buy a modem, and learn how to use it. In fact, the best time to start using a modem is when you're learning about computers for the first time.

That's because modems let you communicate with other people. And since those other people obviously own computers, they've probably overcome the same problems you're having right now. People who "hang out" on computer bulletin boards usually love to swap tech talk; somebody will almost always help to solve your computing problems.

Computer Bulletin Board Systems

Computer Bulletin Board Systems (BBSs) are merely computers connected to the phone lines with a modem. They're usually run by hobbyists, computer nerds, or both.

Members of the public dial up the BBS, connect to the other computer, and use their own keyboard to type in a message. They can talk about the weather, complain about the slovenly habits of a roommate, or ask about RISC chips.

Once they've posted their message, they can read all the other posted messages, and they can respond to any that sound interesting. Other people will dial up, read, and respond. The ensuing electronic conversation sounds like what you'd hear if Radio Shack served mixed drinks as well as capacitors.

Prompt Dialing

Ever wished you had an auto-dialer? If your modem and phone use the same telephone jack, your modem can auto-dial. If your modem's hooked up to your computer's COM1 port, then switch it on and type this at the DOS prompt:

ECHO ATDT555-1212 > COM1

Replace 555-1212 with the number you want to dial. When you hear the line start to ring through your modem's speaker, pick up your phone's handset, then type this line at your keyboard:

ECHO AT > COM1

Modem Magic

This command hangs up the modem, but not the phone. (This only works for voice calls; you can't call a BBS.) To further automate the process, type in the following batch file:

```
@ECHO OFF
IF $%1==$ GOTO FORGOT
ECHO This program dials a phone number.
ECHO Make sure your modem's plugged
ECHO into the phone line and ready to go.
PAUSE
ECHO Dialing %1
ECHO ATDT%1 > COM1
ECHO When phone rings, pick up extension, then press any key.
PAUSE
ECHO AT > COM1
GOTO END
:FORGOT
ECHO Please specify a phone number
ECHO after DIAL, and try again.
:END
```

Save the file under the name DIAL.BAT. Then type "DIAL 555-1212", and your computer will dutifully dial.

What's the Cost?

The best thing about most local boards comes with the price: They're free. The owners of the BBS, staunch hobbyists to their own financial detriment, rarely charge fees to access their system.

Instead, many BBS operators take pride in having a large number of callers. To lure them in, they'll offer free software downloads—you can copy programs from their computer onto your computer.

You won't find programs like *WordPerfect*; instead, you'll find "public domain" or "shareware" programs, which means you can try them out for free. If you find yourself using a shareware program regularly, you should send a small contribution to the author, whose address comes with the program. There's no charge for public domain programs.

Internal or External?

Should you buy a modem that plugs into a slot inside your computer, or one that sits outside your computer, in its own box? Buy the external, even though it will cost a few more dollars.

External modems have a set of lights along the front. The lights let you know when the modems have picked up the phone, whether information is flowing back and forth, if the other modem has answered the call, and give other indicators of the call's progress.

With an internal modem, you can't tell *what's* going on, leading to even more confusion.

Prodigy: A Commercial BBS With Commercials

If you don't mind spending a few dollars for information, check out some of the commercial on-line systems. Beginners might want to try Prodigy, the $13-a-month shopping service started by IBM and Sears. It's easy to set up and install; just follow the simple, step-by-step directions. (It's only available for IBM-compatible and Macintosh computers, by the way.)

The Prodigy screen looks different from most on-line services. It contains colorful pictures, simple animation, and easy, "push-button" menus for easy navigation. In fact, Prodigy is easier to use than programming a VCR. Since the service is so graphics-intensive, it's also a little slower than most, but you get used to it.

Prodigy can also be customized. Once you decide on which of the more than 800 areas you're interested in, you can tell Prodigy to whisk you quickly through those same areas whenever you call.

I use Prodigy almost daily to check out the latest news and weather. Then I jump to the computer games section to read about new games. (I wrote a book on computer games, and the information helped me keep track of recent releases.) Then I check out Prodigy's listing of San Diego events to see what's happening around town. If I wanted, I could also check out ski reports, business news, stock quotes, Consumer Reports, or read columns dealing with wine, music, restaurants, sports, movies, and other topics.

If I had any money, I could book airline and hotel reservations, make rental car arrangements, or order retail goods, like car phones or blue jeans, all billed to my credit card.

Prodigy contains plenty of information and services, but another on-line service, CompuServe, contains much more. It also costs much more: CompuServe charges more than $12 an hour as opposed to Prodigy's $13 a month.

Have an esoteric hobby? You'll find it being discussed on CompuServe. You can ask kinky questions on the Human Sexuality forum. Hang out with fish fanatics on the Aquaria forum. You can find people who are using the same computer you use, no matter how much of a dinosaur it might be. Since they're "hanging around" on-line, they'll be willing and eager to share computing tips.

Have questions about your software package? You can get answers from software forums run by Borland International, Ashton-Tate, WordPerfect and others. Just type in your question, and an answer will be waiting for you, usually within 48 hours.

CompuServe even has a fax service. Use your modem to send CompuServe your document, and they'll send it to the fax machine of your choice for a small fee.

SECRET: Call Waiting

Here's a secret: The "Call Waiting" feature beeps during a conversation to let you know somebody else is calling. This upsets your computer, and the modems will hang up on each other.

To stop this, turn call waiting off before dialing. Touch tone phone users can insert the code "*70" (without the quotes) directly before the phone number, like this: "*70555-5555". If you have pulse dialing, substitute the numbers "1170" for "*70".

If your phone company doesn't offer a "cancel Call Waiting" feature, ask for "Call Forwarding." Then, before each outgoing modem call, forward any incoming calls to your own number: The caller will get a busy signal, and you won't get a beep.

Just make sure to turn off Call Forwarding when you're through, or you won't receive any incoming calls.

Serious researchers will make use of CompuServe's extensive collection of databases, known as "IQuest." The additional database user fee is not cheap, but IQuest is thorough, and it's relatively easy to use. IQuest contains more than 800 publications, databases, and indices. It contains information on business, government, research, marketing, news, and entertainment, including sports and lifestyle publications.

Some publications, like *Newsweek* and *Sports Illustrated*, reach back for 25 years. The databases contain text only, so there's no use searching for the swimsuit issue. But then again, there's no longer any reason to save stacks of magazines in the garage: it's all available through your computer, modem, and phone lines.

If you're not satisfied with Prodigy or CompuServe, plenty of other on-line databases contain just about everything you can think of. For instance, DataTimes carries the complete text from 640 newspapers, magazines, news services and financial data sources from four continents.

If *The San Diego Union* printed one of your letters to the editor, you can read it again on DataTimes (*Union* coverage started in January, '86). DataTimes is a powerful research tool, but it carries a powerful price: more than $1 a minute, in addition to a monthly surcharge of up to $95.

DataTimes is quick, once you've figured out how to use it. It's also expensive, but then again, DataTimes might be the only way to extract a hidden piece of information.

Yet another on-line service, the Sierra Network, lets you play games on-line. It's graphics-based, like Prodigy, but better: You can even draw a picture of yourself to show people on-line. It's one of the most fun on-line services.

A modem isn't always wonderful. In fact, telecommunications can sometimes be a giant headache. I'd heartily recommend looking at Jim Kimble's book, *How to Get Started With Modems*. The $8.95 book is an easy-to-read guide to the on-line world, and it's available at Waldenbooks, Software ETC., or other retailers.

Computer wizard Kimble knows what he's talking about.

Modem Magic

> **SECRET: Don't Pass Out Your Password**
>
> Only good passwords can block out snoopers. Passwords like "sex," "secret," or "OpenSesame" simply don't work. Snoops try those passwords first. Common personal names like "John" and "Mary" rank as second worst. Everybody should choose secure, hard-to-guess passwords.
>
> One secret is to take the first letters of the words in a phrase, like "I Work at Digital Widgets." Very few people will guess the password "IWADW."

Formerly *ComputorEdge* Magazine's On-Line San Diego columnist, Kimble's now slaving away aboard cruise ships, programming their computerized bingo games.

It's never too soon to enter the world of telecommunications. With a modem, you can find an extensive library, a shopping mall, or a conversation-filled bar—all without leaving your home.

How to Make the First Call

Your modem probably came with some sort of telecommunications software, and that's all you need to get started. Plug a phone cord from the wall to the phone jack on your modem; that's all you have to do with an internal modem. External modems need a cable to connect them to the computer's serial port.

When you've connected to a bulletin board, it will usually ask for your name. Type it in. If the board doesn't recognize you, it will ask you to register as a new user. That means you must fill out your name, address and phone number, so the system's owner knows who's calling his system.

Sooner or later, you'll have problems getting the darn setup to work correctly with a certain board (or any board, when just starting!). Luckily, modem maniacs love to help beginners work through the process.

See you on-line!

CHAPTER 10

Tips on Disks

The computer world thrives on three main types of disks: floppy disks, hard disks (or drives), and compact discs. All of them do pretty much the same thing: They store information for your computer to play with.

Floppy Disks

Floppy disks come in two sizes, 5¼ and 3½ inches. Each of those two sizes comes in two flavors, high or low density, with high-density disks holding the largest amount of data.

Newer computers, like the AT, started using high-density disks and drives, which can pack a lot more information into the same space. If you're using one of these newer drives, be sure to buy the high-density disks. (Unfortunately, they're more expensive than their low-density counterparts.)

Regardless of a disk's size or density, disks don't work when they come straight out of the box. You must format them first, and it's pretty easy. To format a floppy in the A: drive, type FORMAT A: and hit the <Enter> key. If you're formatting a low-density disk in a high-density drive, you'll need to add a few commands. See the following page for a handy chart.

When buying your computer, choose the high-density drives,

IBM PC Formatted Capacity	Diskette Size	Comments	Format Command In Low-Density Drive A	Format Command In High-Density Drive A
360K	5¼ inch	Double Sided/ Double Density	Format A:	Format A:/4
720K	3½ inch	Double Sided/ Double Density	Format A:	Format A:/n:9/t:80
1.2 MB	5¼ inch	Double Sided/ High Capacity	—	Format A:
1.4 MB	3½ inch	Double Sided/ High Capacity	—	Format A:

because they can access both high- and low-density disks. Buy one 5¼-inch drive and one 3½-inch drive, and you'll be able to handle any disk. (Except the weird new 2-inch disks used in some laptops and portable cameras.)

How can you tell whether you have a high-density or low-density disk? Look at the 3½-inch disk: If there's a small square hole on both the left and right sides of the top edge, it's high density. If there's only a hole on the top-right side, it's low density. Unfortunately, there's no way to determine the densities of the 5¼-inch disks. Both varieties look identical. If you're lucky, it will tell you on the label.

SECRET: A = B

If you have a floppy drive and a hard drive, your floppy drive will be A: and your hard drive will be C:, right?

Well, sometimes. Your computer always thinks it has two floppy drives, even if you've only purchased one. If you try to copy something from your C: drive to your A: drive, it will work fine. If you try to copy it to a non-existent B: drive, your computer will pause and ask you to stick a disk in drive B:. Just hit <Enter>, and you'll be fine.

SECRET: Punching a Hole in the Theory

Sooner or later someone will tell you to punch a hole in a 3½-inch disk so it will hold more data. That's because disk drives look for a hole in the disk casing to determine whether the disk is double-sided or single-sided (and whether it's double density or high density).

By punching that extra hole, you can fool the computer into thinking it's using a more expensive disk that can hold more data.

The good news is that the trick often works. The bad news is that there's a reason the double-sided disks are less expensive. The cheaper disks couldn't handle any higher data capacity during the disk testing process.

So when the modified disk crashes, ruining your important data, the fact that you've saved some spare change won't make you feel any better. Don't do it.

Write-Protection

When you copy important files to disk, you should "write-protect" the disk, so you won't accidentally "overwrite" any important files.

To write-protect the 5¼-inch disk, look for the little black or silver stickers that came with the box. Then fold one little sticker over the edge of the disk, covering that square notch cut in the side near the label.

If you've lost the special stickers, masking tape will often work just as well.

To write-protect the 3½-inch disks, look for a small square hole in the disk's top corner. You'll find a small black "window" next to it that can be open or shut by pushing it with a pen or pencil. When the window's open, the floppy disk is write-protected.

To protect your data even further, make two backup copies of all disks. Keep one near the computer for reference, and keep another at work, or at a friend's house. That way you'll have your data, even if your house burns down.

Care and Feeding

Floppy disks hold up well to abuse, but that doesn't mean they're masochists. Follow these tips to keep you both happy:

- Never touch the inside of the disk. Don't open the door on the 3½-inch disk to peek inside, and don't touch the exposed disk surface on the 5¼-inchers.

- Write the disk's contents on the sticky labels that came in the box. In a pinch, use address labels. Without a label, you'll never find your backup copies. Don't use anything but a felt-tipped pen to write on the label of a 5¼-inch disk; sharp pens and pencils can cause damage. Finally, you might have to peel off the old labels before putting on new ones; occasionally they'll get too thick to fit in the drive!

- Keep the disks away from magnets or magnetic fields. Keep them away from any speakers or radios you may have on your desk; watch out for paper-clip holders, telephones, electric pencil sharpeners, or anything with a motor.

- The x-ray machines at airports don't bother computers or disks, but make sure the laptop bag doesn't drag near the floor. Disks can be damaged by the motors that power the conveyor belt.

SECRET: Gunning for Success

Why are hard drives sometimes called Winchester drives? They're named after the man who built and sold thousands of Winchester repeating rifles back in the Old West. In the earlier days of computing, tech types got together and set a goal: They'd build a hard drive capable of holding 30 MB of data, and accessing that data in 30 milliseconds. That 30/30 project bore the same name as the Winchester 30/30 rifle created a century before. After all, *Star Trek* was a Western, too.

Tips on Disks

- Keep disks in their dust jackets to protect them from dirt and grime. Keep them away from extreme heat or cold. Don't leave them on windowsills, or on your car's dashboard.

Hard Disks

Hard disks and hard drives are two names for the same thing: thick disks that spin inside your computer and hold more information than hundreds of floppies. Sometimes they're called Winchester drives.

In this day of immediate gratification, it's bothersome to fiddle with floppies every time you want to run a program. Hard drives allow instant access to all your programs and data. Many newer programs, including those written for *Windows*, won't even fit on a floppy. One program, *Word for Windows* v.2, takes up 15 MB of space. Try fitting that on a floppy!

When shopping for a hard drive, buy one that's twice the size you think you'll need. It'll fill up faster than you think. And with that much storage space, organization becomes very important.

Organizing Your Hard Drive
File Names

You can get away with tossing a few files onto a floppy and labeling the disk "letters." But a hard drive holds many hiding places

---

Secret: Secret Files

Remember the secret in Chapter Five about using the <Alt> key and the numeric keypad to create characters? You can use the same trick to name files. Check out this file name: πΓΛθ.TXT.

You can keep out snoops by putting one of these strange characters in the filename. They won't be able to use DOS's TYPE command to type out its contents. You can even use the <Alt-255> key combination to make the file name two words. Just remember to use <Alt-255>, not the space bar, when accessing the file later.

for files. Your only recourse is to name files something you can remember later. Don't call the file "STUFF"; call it "CHAPTER1.TXT" or something specific.

DOS lets you devote eight characters to the first part of the name, along with a three letter extension. Use the extension wisely. For instance, end your word processing files with the extension DOC or TXT. Call your project's notes PROJECT.NTS; call the project PROJECT.TXT.

Help! I Deleted a File

Quick! Turn to Chapter Four and read about the UNDELETE utility that came with DOS 5.0. Don't have DOS 5.0? Then pick up a copy of *Norton Utilities*, or some other utility package. They'll help you with other hard disk maintenance chores described in Chapter Four.

Backups

Just as it's important to back up your floppies, you must back up your hard drive. It's a chore, regardless of the method you use. Most versions of DOS come with a backup program, or you can use one of the commercial packages.

To make your backup process easier, partition your hard drive into two sections, calling them C: and D:. Some people keep all their programs on C:, and all their data on D:. That way they'll only have to back up their D: drive, because that's the only section that will be constantly changing. The C: drive will be backed up on the original program disks.

Directories

A hard drive can be broken down into separate folders, called "directories." By saving files in separate directories, it's much easier to find them later. Too many people just dump everything in their "root" directory, that familiar "C:\>" prompt.

But this slows the computer. Every time you type a command, it

Tips on Disks

searches through every file in your root directory trying to find that program. Keep only three files in your root directory, and your computer won't have to search as long.

Keep your AUTOEXEC.BAT file, your CONFIG.SYS file, and your COMMAND.COM file in your root directory. Everything else should be squared away. For instance, create a WORDS directory for your word processing by typing MD WORDS from your C:\> prompt.

Secret: Staying in Fashion

Your computer's CONFIG.SYS and AUTOEXEC.BAT files tell your computer what it's wearing and what it's supposed to do when it wakes up. But since software has become so demanding in terms of memory and other hardware, you'll often find yourself editing those files to make your computer happy.

There's a better way. For instance, let's say you want a special set of CONFIG.SYS files and an AUTOEXEC.BAT file for *Windows*. Create a CONFIG.SYS file with all your *Windows* drivers, and an AUTOEXEC.BAT file that will boot up *Windows* from the beginning. Name these files CONFIG.WIN and AUTOEXEC.WIN, and store them in your utility directory.

Then take your normal CONFIG.SYS and AUTOEXEC.BAT files and store a copy of them in your utility directory. Call the copies: CONFIG.NRM and AUTOEXEC.NRM. (The "NRM" means "normal.")

Finally, write this *Windows* batch file:

COPY C:\UTILITY\CONFIG.WIN C:\CONFIG.SYS
COPY C:\UTILITY\AUTOEXEC.WIN C:\AUTOEXEC.BAT

Save this file in your utility directory as AUTOWIN.BAT. Now, when you type AUTOWIN, your computer will dress itself for *Windows*. Reboot, and you'll be ready to run in the *Windows* environment. Create a "Normal" batch file that copies the "NRM" files over the WIN files in the root directory; then type AUTONORM and reboot to use your computer without *Windows*.

Make separate AUTO files for each of the picky programs you need to use.

Then, divide the WORDS subdirectory into separate subdirectories to hold even more data. Make a subdirectory for each project, no matter how small, and you'll be able to find your information much more quickly.

Compression Systems

Your 40 MB hard drive may seem big enough when you buy it, but that feeling won't last. Hard drives always fill up too quickly. But before you buy a new hard drive, check out one of the new "disk compression" programs. They can often double your drive's storage capacity.

AddStor's *SuperStor* and Stac Electronics' *Stacker*, can turn a 30 MB drive into a 60 MB drive. Unlike PKZIP and ARJ (discussed in Chapter Four), these programs operate invisibly. The programs automatically compress every file on your hard disk, giving you extra space.

Then you work normally; the programs automatically decompress the files as they're needed. And they work so quickly, you'll barely notice what's going on.

When you're finished using files, the compression programs squeeze them back down to save space. How much space? That depends on the files. Text files can compress the most; programs don't compress very much at all.

For more information, contact the following companies:

- *SuperStor* ($129)
  AddStor, Inc.
  3905 Bohannon Drive
  Menlo Park, CA 94025
  (415) 688-0470

- *Stacker* ($149, Software)
  ($229, Software and Coprocessor Board)
  Stac Electronics
  5993 Avenida Encinas
  Carlsbad, CA 92008
  (800) 522-7822

APPENDICES

APPENDIX A

All About ASCII Characters

Control Characters

These are the characters produced by holding down the <Ctrl> key and simultaneously hitting another key. The number before each character is the decimal value the computer has assigned that character. With a different decimal value for each character, the computer won't become confused between <m>, <M>, and <^M> , for instance. (The caret symbol, ^, represents the <Ctrl> key.) To create any of the characters in these tables, you can type in the decimal number with the keypad while holding down the <Alt> key. See Chapter Five for more details.

Control characters aren't part of the alphabet. Instead, they're used as signals to tell the software what to do. Pushing <^K> for instance, can pull up a word processing menu.

```
 0 ^@    1 ^A    2 ^B    3 ^C    4 ^D    5 ^E    6 ^F    7 ^G
 8 ^H    9 ^I   10 ^J   11 ^K   12 ^L   13 ^M   14 ^N   15 ^O
16 ^P   17 ^Q   18 ^R   19 ^S   20 ^T   21 ^U   22 ^V   23 ^W
24 ^X   25 ^Y   26 ^Z   27 ^[   28 ^\   29 ^]   30 ^^   31 ^_
```

Standard Text Characters

These are the characters you'll see in your documents. They're the alphabet, the numbers, and a few common symbols. What's the character accessed by the blank left next to number 32? That's the spacebar!

```
 32      33 !  34 π  35 #  36 $  37 %  38 &  39 ʖ
 40 (   41 )  42 *  43 +  44 ,  45 -  46 .  47 /
 48 0   49 1  50 2  51 3  52 4  53 5  54 6  55 7
 56 8   57 9  58 :  59 ;  60 <  61 =  62 >  63 ?
 64 @   65 A  66 B  67 C  68 D  69 E  70 F  71 G
 72 H   73 I  74 J  75 K  76 L  77 M  78 N  79 O
 80 P   81 Q  82 R  83 S  84 T  85 U  86 V  87 W
 88 X   89 Y  90 Z  91 [  92 \  93 ]  94 ^  95 _
 96 `   97 a  98 b  99 c 100 d 101 e 102 f 103 g
104 h  105 i 106 j 107 k 108 l 109 m 110 n 111 o
112 p  113 q 114 r 115 s 116 t 117 u 118 v 119 w
120 x  121 y 122 z 123 { 124 | 125 } 126 ~ 127 ⌂
```

Extended ASCII Characters

Here you'll find your foreign characters. They'll change according to what "code page" you've assigned to your country setting. (See Chapter Five.)

```
128 Ç 129 ü 130 é 131 â 132 ä 133 à 134 à 135 ç
136 ê 137 ë 138 è 139 ï 140 î 141 ì 142 Ä 143 Å
144 É 145 æ 146 Æ 147 ô 148 ö 149 ò 150 û 151 ù
152 ÿ 153 Ö 154 Ü 155 ¢ 156 £ 157 ¥ 158 ₧ 159 ƒ
160 á 161 í 162 ó 163 ú 164 ñ 165 Ñ 166 ª 167 º
168 ¿ 169 ⌐ 170 ¬ 171 ½ 172 ¼ 173 ¡ 174 « 175 »
176 ░ 177 ▒ 178 ▓ 179 │ 180 ┤ 181 ╡ 182 ╢ 183 ╖
184 ╕ 185 ╣ 186 ║ 187 ╗ 188 ╝ 189 ╜ 190 ╛ 191 ┐
192 └ 193 ┴ 194 ┬ 195 ├ 196 ─ 197 ┼ 198 ╞ 199 ╟
200 ╚ 201 ╔ 202 ╩ 203 ╦ 204 ╠ 205 ═ 206 ╬ 207 ╧
208 ╨ 209 ╤ 210 ╥ 211 ╙ 212 ╘ 213 ╒ 214 ╓ 215 ╫
216 ╪ 217 ┘ 218 ┌ 219 █ 220 ▄ 221 ▌ 222 ▐ 223 ▀
224 α 225 β 226 Γ 227 π 228 Σ 229 σ 230 µ 231 τ
232 Φ 233 Θ 234 Ω 235 δ 236 ∞ 237 φ 238 ∈ 239 ∩
240 ≡ 241 ± 242 ≥ 243 ≤ 244 ⌠ 245 ⌡ 246 ÷ 247 ≈
248 ° 249 · 250 · 251 √ 252 ⁿ 253 ² 254 ■ 255
```

ASCII

Control Character Names

You'll probably never need to know these, but they're handy to have. For instance, Decimal 7, <^G>, and BEL are "Bell," or the "beep" you hear when you do something wrong. To hear the beep, type ECHO <^G> at the DOS prompt and hit <Enter>. Your computer will beep.

Similarly, you can control your printer using the ECHO trick and some of these characters.

```
0   ^@  NUL  Null                  16  ^P  DLE  Data Link Escape
1   ^A  SOH  Start of Heading      17  ^Q  DC1  Device Control 1
2   ^B  STX  Start of Text         18  ^R  DC2  Device Control 2
3   ^C  ETX  End of Text           19  ^S  DC3  Device Control 3
4   ^D  EOT  End of Transmission   20  ^T  DC4  Device Control 4
5   ^E  ENQ  Enquiry               21  ^U  NAK  Negative Acknowledgement
6   ^F  ACK  Acknowledge           22  ^V  SYN  Synchronous File
7   ^G  BEL  Bell                  23  ^W  ETB  End of Transmission Block
8   ^H  BS   Backspace             24  ^X  CAN  Cancel
9   ^I  HT   Horizontal Tab        25  ^Y  EM   End of Medium
10  ^J  LF   Line Feed             26  ^Z  SUB  Substitute
11  ^K  VT   Vertical Tab          27  ^[  ESC  Escape
12  ^L  FF   Form Feed             28  ^\  FS   Form Separator
13  ^M  CR   Carriage Return       29  ^]  GS   Group Separator
14  ^N  SO   Shift Out             30  ^^  RS   Record Separator
15  ^O  SI   Shift In              31  ^_  US   Unit Separator
```

For more information about ASCII characters, check out Dan Gookin's *DOS Secrets*. You'll find ordering information in the back of this book.

APPENDIX B

Basic Command Set

Modem Command Set

Your modem talks in this language, the AT command set. To get its attention, you type AT into your terminal program. If you hit <Enter>, your modem will respond "OK." Almost every modem on the market will recognize these AT commands; they're based on a modem made by a company called Hayes. That company set a standard for modem language that everybody else is following.

When you turn on your modem, it "defaults" to a certain "Hayes" setting. You can change any of the settings by typing "AT", and the value you want to change. For instance, "ATH0" means to hang up the phone.

These are the basic commands. Your modem will have many more listed in its manual as an "extended" command set. These will differ from modem to modem, so there's no point in listing them here. These extended commands will let you take advantage of special features built into particular modems.

For more information about modems, check out Jim Kimble's book, *How to Get Started With Modems*. You'll find ordering information in the back of this book.

Command	Options/Function
A	Force Answer Mode when modem hasn't received an incoming call.
A/	Re-execute the last command.
A>	Re-execute the last command (redial) continuously.
Any key	Terminate current dialing operation resulting from issued Dial command.
AT	Attention: must precede all other commands, except A/, A> and +++.
B*n*	U.S./CCITT answer sequence. B0 CCITT answer sequence B1 U.S., Canada answer tone—Default.
C*n*	Transmitter enabled/disabled. C0 Transmitter disabled. C1 Transmitter enabled—Default.
D*n*	Dial the number (n) that follows and go into Originate Mode. Use any of the following options: P Pulse dial—Default. T Touch-Tone dial. , (Comma) Pause for 2 seconds. ; Return to command state after dialing. " Dial the letters that follow. ! Flash switch-hook to transfer call. W Wait for second dial tone (if X3 or higher is set). @ Wait for an answer (if X3 or higher is set). R Reverse frequencies.

Basic Command Set

Command	Options/Function
DS*n*	Dial number (n = 0—3) stored in NRAM.
E*n*	Command Mode local echo: display copy of modem commands entered at the keyboard. If your modem doesn't say "OK" after you type AT<Enter>, type "ATE1" to turn on the echo. (Not applicable once a connection has been made.) E0 Echo OFF. E1 Echo ON.
F*n*	Local echo ON/OFF once a connection has been established. F0 Echo ON. F1 Echo OFF—Default.
H*n*	On/off hook control. H0 Hang up (go on hook)—Default. H1 Go off hook.
I*n*	Inquiry. I0 Return product code. I1 Return memory (ROM) checksum. I2 Run memory (RAM) test. I3 Return call duration/real time. I4 Return current modem settings. I5 Return NRAM settings.
K*n*	Modem clock operation. K0 At AT13, display call duration—Default. K1 At AT13, display real time; set clock with AT13 = HH:MM:SSK1.
M*n*	Monitor (speaker) control. M0 Speaker always OFF. M1 Speaker ON until carrier is established—Default.

Command	Options/Funtion
	M2 Speaker always ON.
	M3 Speaker ON after last digit dialed, OFF at carrier detect.
O	Return on-line after command execution.
P	Pulse dial.
Q*n*	Quiet Mode: result codes displayed/suppressed.
	Q0 Result codes displayed.
	Q1 Result codes suppressed.
S*r*=*n*	Set Register commands: *r* is any. S-register, *n* must be a decimal number between 0 and 255.
S*r*?	Query S-register *r*. (See next page)
T	Tone dial.
V*n*	Verbal/Numeric result codes.
	V0 Numeric Mode.
	V1 Verbal Mode.
X*n*	Result Code options. Use the Options Table on this reference card. Default is X1, Extended set, codes 0-5, 10.
Z	Reset modem to defaults.
+++	Escape code sequence, preceded and followed by at least one second of no data transmission.
>	Repeat command continuously or up to 10 dial attempts. (Cancel by pressing any key.)
/	(Slash) Pause for 125 msec.
$	Help command summary.

Basic Command Set *117*

Command	Options/Function
&$	Help Extended command summary.
D$	Help Dial command summary.
S$	Help S-register summary.

> **SECRET: Speed**
> Put the command ATS11=55 in your modem string to speed up dialing on most modems!

S Registers

The AT commands are toggle switches for your modem, in that they turn a feature, like auto-answer, on or off. But sometimes you'll want to move beyond on/off information; you might want to store a number in your modem, like the amount of time it should wait before starting to dial.

That's when you use an "S" register. You set the S registers with an AT command. For instance, the command ATS6=2 means the modem will wait 2 seconds before dialing. Here's a list of the most important S registers for a US Robotics 2400e modem. Your own list might vary, depending on your modem.

S0 Number of rings to wait before auto-answering.
S1 Counts and stores number of rings from an incoming call.
S6 Number of seconds the modem waits before dialing.
S7 Number of seconds the modem waits for the dial tone.
S8 The number of seconds the modem pauses for the <,> command.
S10 The time in tenth of a seconds, the modem will wait before hanging up after the carrier drops.
S11 The number of milliseconds between tones when dialing.

APPENDIX C

Country CodePage Chart

COUNTRY=CountryCode [,CodePage] [,pathname]

These three-digit numbers identify the desired country code. The system will boot up with COUNTRY=001 if you don't tell it otherwise. The CodePage usually isn't important, as it will start with the most common one for that language.

    001   United States
    002   French-Canadian
    003   Latin American
    031   Netherlands
    032   Belgium
    033   France
    034   Spain
    036   Hungary
    038   Yugoslavia
    039   Italy
    041   Switzerland
    042   Czechoslovakia
    044   United Kingdom
    045   Denmark
    046   Sweden
    047   Norway
    048   Poland

Country CodePage Chart

049 Germany
055 Brazil
061 International English
081 Japan (only with special versions of MS-DOS)
082 Korea (only with special versions of MS-DOS)
086 China (only with special versions of MS-DOS)
088 Taiwan (only with special versions of MS-DOS)
351 Portugal
358 Finland
785 Arabic (only with special versions of MS-DOS)
972 Israel (only with special versions of MS-DOS)

These three-digit numbers correspond to the codepage, which in turn, correspond to the country code.

437 United States
850 Multilingual
852 Slavic
860 Portuguese
863 French Canadian
865 Nordic

(Fill in the [pathname] box with the subdirectory containing your COUNTRY.SYS file.)

APPENDIX D

Telecommunications Services

Here's how to reach the customer service departments of several on-line services. Call using your voice, not your modem, and the friendly operator will give you ordering information.

America Online	800-227-6364
BIX	603-924-7681
BRS/Search	800-468-0908
BRS/After Dark	800-468-0908
CompuServe	800-848-8199
Data Times	800-642-2525
Delphi	800-544-4005
Dow Jones News Retrieval	609-452-1511
GEnie	800-638-9636
DIALOG	800-334-2564
Knowledge Index	800-334-2564
Prodigy	800-PRODIGY
Sierra Network	800-SIERRA-1
The Well	415-332-4335
MCI Mail	800-444-6245
AT&T Mail	800-624-5672

INDEX

Index

A

addresses, 86
America Online, 121
ANSI codes, 57
ANSI.SYS, 56
ASCII, 13, 109
   control characters, 109
   extended characters, 110
   standard text characters, 110
ASCII files, 14
AT&T Mail, 121
auto-dialer, 92
AUTOEXEC.BAT, 15, 105

B

back door, 12, 31
backups, 104
basic command set, 113
Basic Input/Output System
   see also BIOS, 12
batch files, 18
BBS, 92
   cost, 93
BIOS, 12
BIX, 121
boards, 80
boot, 11
BRS/After Dark, 121
BRS/Search, 121
bulletin board system
   see also BBS, 92

C

call waiting, 95
CapsLock, 53
cards, 80
   addresses, 86
   fax/modem, 85
   installation, 80
   interrupt, 87
   memory, 86
   port conflicts, 86
   problems, 85
   scanners, 85
   sound, 84
   types of, 82
   video, 86
CGA, 64
codepage, 120
Color Graphics Adapter
   see also CGA, 64
COMMAND.COM, 14
compression systems, 106
   Stacker, 106
   SuperStor, 106
CompuServe, 95, 121
   IQuest, 96
CONFIG.SYS, 13, 105
control characters, 109, 111
Control Room, 51
conventional DOS memory, 4
country codes, 119
CPU, 3
Ctrl (Control), 52
Ctrl-Alt-Del, 53
Ctrl-C, 52
Ctrl-G, 52
Ctrl-P, 53
Ctrl-S, 52

D

DataTimes, 96, 121
defragment, 43
Delphi, 121
DIALOG, 121
directories, 104
Disk Analysis, 44
disks, 99
   care of, 102
   floppy, 99
   hard, 103
   sizes, 99
   write-protection, 101

DOS, 3
  conventional DOS memory, 4
  high DOS memory, 6
  shell, 19
  tips, 11
Doskey, 41
Dosshell, 41
dot matrix printers, 71
dot pitch, 66
Dow Jones News Retrieval, 121
drives, 100

E

EGA, 64
EMM, 7
EMS, 7
enhanced mode, 9
Esc (Escape), 52
expanded memory, 7
expansion boards, 79
expansion bus, 80
extended ASCII characters, 110
Extended Graphics Adapter
  see also EGA, 64
extended memory, 7
extensions, 30

F

fax/modem, 85
file dates, 21
  changing, 21
foreign characters, 110
foreign language characters, 55
function keys, 54

G

GEnie, 121
GeoWorks, 24
Graphical User Interface
  see also GUI, 26
GUI, 26

H

hard disks, 103
hard drive, 103
  backup, 104
  compression systems, 106
  directories, 104
  organization, 103
high DOS memory, 6
hot key, 4

I

impact printers, 73
inkjet printers, 73
interrupts, 86
invisible files, 13
IQuest, 96

K

keyboard
  AT, 48
  Dvorak, 49
  enhanced, 50, 101
  tips, 47
  tricks, 55
  XT, 48
Knowledge Index, 121

L

laser printers, 74

M

macros, 51
MCI Mail, 121
memory
  EMM, 7
  EMS, 7
  expanded, 7
  extended, 7
  managers, 9
memory cards, 86
memory-resident, 4
  TSR, 5

Index

menu
  creating, 57
modems, 91
  call waiting, 95
  command set, 113
  command table, 114
  country codes, 119
  external, 94
  internal, 94
  passwords, 97
  prompt dialing, 92
  S registers, 117
  speed, 117
  your first call, 97
monitors, 63
  cards, 65
  CGA, 64
  color, 63
  color choices, 64
  EGA, 64
  line size, 69
  monochrome, 63
  screen savers, 67
  super VGA, 64
  terms, 66
  trouble-shooting, 67
  VGA, 64
MS-DOS, 3

N

Norton Utilities, 43
NumLock, 53

O

on-line services, 121
  America Online, 121
  CompuServe, 95, 121
  DataTimes, 96, 121
  Genie, 121
  Prodigy, 94, 121
  Sierra Network, 96, 121

open architecture, 79
operating systems, 23
  GeoWorks, 24
  OS/2, 23
  UNIX, 23
  Windows, 24
  Xenix, 23
optimize, 43
OS/2, 23
output redirection, 38

P

path, 16
  modifying, 16
pause the directory, 20
PC Tools, 43
pixels, 66
PKUNZIP, 46
port conflicts, 86
PostScript, 75
print spoolers, 76
printers, 71
  dot matrix, 71
  impact, 73
  inkjet, 73
  laser, 74
  thermal, 74
Prodigy, 94, 121
prompt, 15
  modifying, 15
  samples, 17
prompt dialing, 92
public domain, 44

Q

QEMM, 9

R

RAM, 3
RAM disk, 8
RAM drive, 8

Random-Access Memory
  see also RAM, 3
Read-Only Memory
  see also ROM, 12
real mode, 9
resolution, 66
ROM, 12

S

S registers, 117
S-VGA, 64
scanners, 85
screen savers, 67
Scroll Lock, 53
secret files, 103
SHARE, 32
shell, 19
Sierra Network, 96, 121
slots, 80
  choice of, 83
sound cards, 84
special keys, 51
  CapsLock, 53
  Ctrl, 52
  Ctrl-Alt-Del, 53
  Ctrl-C, 52
  Ctrl-G, 52
  Ctrl-P, 53
  Ctrl-S, 52
  Esc, 52
  function keys, 54
  NumLock, 53
  Scroll Lock, 53
  SysRq, 53
Stacker, 106
standard text characters, 110
super VGA
  see also S-VGA, 64
SuperStor, 106
SysRq, 53

T

telecommunications services
  see on-line services, 121
The Well, 121
thermal printers, 74
TSR, 5
  trouble-shooting, 5

U

UAE, 32
UNIX, 23
unrecoverable application error, 32
upper DOS memory, 6
utilities, 37
  CHKDSK.COM, 38
  compression, 46
  Control Room, 51
  Doskey, 41
  Dosshell, 41
  EDIT, 42
  LABEL.COM, 39
  MORE, 39
  Norton Utilities, 43
  PC Tools, 43
  public domain, 44
  SETVER, 42
  SORT.EXE, 40
  UNDELETE, 43
  where to find, 45

V

VGA, 64
video cards, 86
Video Graphics Array
  see also VGA, 64

W

wallpaper, 27
Winchester drives, 102

Index

Windows, 24
  bugs, 32
  customizing, 29
  extensions, 30
  GUI, 26
  key equivalents, 30
  program manager, 33
  screenshots, 31
  system editor, 28
  Tips, 28
  wallpaper, 27
write-protection, 101

X
Xenix, 23

Z
ZIP, 46

Other Books From
Computer Publishing Enterprises:

PC Secrets
Tips and Tricks to Increase Your Computer's Power
by R. Andrew Rathbone

Future Computer Opportunities
Visions of Computers Into the Year 2000
by Jack Dunning

Software Buying Secrets
by Wally Wang

DOS Secrets
by Dan Gookin

101 Computer Business Ideas
by Wally Wang

Digital Dave's Computer Tips and Secrets
A Beginner's Guide to Problem Solving
by Roy Davis

The Best FREE Time-Saving Utilities for the PC
by Wally Wang

How to Get Started With Modems
by Jim Kimble

How to Make Money With Computers
by Jack Dunning

Rookie Programming
A Newcomer's Guide to Programming in BASIC, C, and Pascal
by Ron Dippold

Hundreds of Fascinating and Unique Ways to Use Your Computer
by Tina Rathbone

The Computer Gamer's Bible
by R. Andrew Rathbone

Beginner's Guide to DOS
by Dan Gookin

Computer Entrepreneurs
People Who Built Successful Businesses Around Computers
by Linda Murphy

How to Understand and Buy Computers
By Dan Gookin

Parent's Guide to Educational Software and Computers
by Lynn Stewart and Toni Michael

The Official Computer Widow's (and Widower's) Handbook
by Experts on Computer Widow/Widowerhood

For more information about these books, call 1-800-544-5541.